Robert E. Quinn

Beyond Rational Management

*Mastering the Paradoxes
and Competing Demands
of High Performance*

 Jossey-Bass Publishers

San Francisco   •   Oxford   •   1991

BEYOND RATIONAL MANAGEMENT
Mastering the Paradoxes and Competing Demands of High Performance
by Robert E. Quinn

Copyright © 1988 by: Jossey-Bass Inc., Publishers
350 Sansome Street
San Francisco, California 94104
&
Jossey-Bass Limited
Headington Hill Hall
Oxford OX3 0BW

Don Burr's speech, originally published in "The Transition That Hasn't Happened," by Richard Hackman, in *Managing Organizational Transitions*, edited by John R. Kimberly and Robert E. Quinn, is reprinted by permission. Copyright © 1984, Homewood, Ill., Dow Jones-Irwin.

The Steve Thompson Story, originally published by Dow Jones-Irwin in *Managing the Corporate Dream* by William R. Torbert, is reprinted by permission. Copyright © 1987 by William R. Torbert.

Excerpts from the article entitled "Bridging Management Practice and Theory," by S. R. Faerman, R. E. Quinn, and M. P. Thompson are reprinted with permission of *Public Administration Review*, copyright © 1987 by the American Society for Public Administration, 1120 G Street, N.W., Suite 500, Washington, D.C. All rights reserved.

Library of Congress Cataloging-in-Publication Data

Quinn, Robert E.
  Beyond rational management.

  (The Jossey-Bass management series)
  Bibliography
  Includes index.
  1. Organizational effectiveness. 2. Executive ability. I. Title. II. Series.
  HD58.9.Q36 1988   658.4'09   87-46339
  ISBN 1-55542-075-3 (alk. paper)
  ISBN 1-55542-377-9 (paperback)

JACKET/COVER DESIGN BY WILLI BAUM

FIRST EDITION

  HB Printing   10 9 8 7 6
  PB Printing   10 9 8 7 6 5 4 3 2 1

Code 8812
Code 9176 (paperback)

The Jossey-Bass Management Series

Contents

8. The Road to Mastery: An Agenda for
    Transforming Your Management Style   110

9. Assessment and Skill-Building Exercises   127

10. Teaching Management Skills Using the
    Competing Values Model: A Case Study   148

    Conclusion: Beyond Rational Management   161

    Resource A. A Competing Values Reading List   166

    Resource B. Competing Values Leadership
    Instrument: Extended Version   174

    Resource C. Interview Questions for Doing a
    Competing Values Organizational Analysis   181

    References   185

    Index   193

Tables, Figures, and Exhibits

Chapter Five

Chapter Six

Chapter Seven

Chapter Eight

Chapter Nine

Chapter Ten

Resource B

Resource C

Preface

There have been many attempts to answer the seemingly simple question "what is an effective manager?" Popular speakers, writers, and consultants regularly address this issue. Some argue that to be effective a manager must take a hard-nosed, dollar-and-cents approach. Others point out the need to care for employees. Some press for innovation and creativity. Still others discuss the importance of documentation, information management, and control. Armed with logical arguments and dramatic stories, these spokespeople are very persuasive. When we listen to one of them we tend to nod our heads in agreement. "Yes," we say, "that is the secret to being an effective manager." Only when we are again confronted by the harsh realities of the in-basket do we stop to realize that management is far more complicated than any of these spokespeople suggest.

Consultants and popular writers are not the only ones who are concerned with the question of managerial effectiveness. Social scientists, armed with sophisticated statistical techniques, have long searched for the variables that predict effectiveness. Their carefully considered and precise analyses have often resulted in complex statements, which, from the perspective of practice, are distant from reality and not very useful. Even among themselves, social scientists are frustrated with their collective inability to agree on what an effective manager is.

Why is it so hard to respond to this question? Because the question itself assumes the possibility of a single, logical answer, by which I mean an internally consistent statement. The question requires an answer that is based on clear assumptions, mutually exclusive categories, and rational argument. While such statements are necessary in order to communicate, they can sometimes be very misleading. They suggest a constancy that does not exist and fail to capture a truth that R.G.H. Siu (1980, p. 3) described eloquently: "The polished manager . . . does not complain that people are not following the rules or are changing their minds while the program is underway. He does not expect that Nature is going to hold the Universe constant, while he goes about making up his plans and pursuing his projections. He recognizes that social dilemmas are not like mathematical problems, which can be solved for all times, like '2 plus 2 equals 4.' There is no such thing as a 'labor problem,' for instance, which can be attacked and settled once and for all. There are only labor issues — never fully defined, gyrating in constant chameleonic flux and defying even semipermanent dispositions."

The world of upper management is indeed "gyrating in constant chameleonic flux." But administrative theory, the prescriptions of consultants, and even the explanations of successful managers fail to reflect this reality. In order to understand managerial effectiveness, we must move beyond the theories of rational management and begin to better understand the dynamic, paradoxical, and competing forces that block us from creating high-performance systems.

Mastery of Contradiction and Paradox

Certainly, highly effective managers are rational, but they are rational in very dynamic and complex ways. In running large organizations, there is no one way to manage effectively. Master managers understand this and develop the capacity to use several contradictory logics simultaneously.

Normally we think of the use of contradictory logics as a sequential process. A strategy is formed and implemented. After a time it is discarded and replaced by another. Sometimes the second strategy is based on a radically different set of assumptions — a shift to another logic, which might involve a change in orientation from task to person, from stability to change, or some other similar turn. From this sequential viewpoint, more perspectives mean more alternatives and a greater likelihood of being effective.

There is another way in which a master manager can use contradictory logics. However, it is much more difficult for us to think about because it involves events that are not sequential but simultaneous. As a manager develops the capacity to use contradictory perspectives, he or she is occasionally able to pursue two or more contradictory notions at the same time. When this happens, solutions to problems tend to be ingenious, and individual and collective performance tends to become highly energized. In the popular parlance, excellence is created.

This process is difficult to think about and understand because it is paradoxical. From our normal perspective, it seems to mix ways of thinking that cannot be combined. From the point of view of our traditional managerial concepts and theories, paradoxes are intolerable. Such theories are oversimplifications that lead us away from the understanding we seek (Van de Ven, 1983).

In *Beyond Rational Management*, I move closer to an understanding of the paradoxical dynamics that underlie effectiveness, mastery, and excellence. I attempt to build a new comprehension of managerial effectiveness — one that transcends the oversimplified concepts that currently serve to both facilitate and limit our understanding.

Frequently, practitioners become dissatisfied with the either/or, hierarchical logic of classical thinking, and occasionally, some theorists respond to this dissatisfaction by differentiating between the two commonly utilized philosophies of management. The old approach is purposive, static, and entropic, while the new one is holistic, dynamic, and generative. A few examples of such differentiations are Theory X and Theory Y (McGregor, 1960), management and leadership (Zaleznik, 1977), and transactional and transformational leadership

(Burns, 1978). Theorists tend to define the new approach as good, or at least better, than the old approach. For example, Theory Y is enlightened management, while Theory X is the approach of a caveman in a tie. In addition to the issue of moral overtones, Theory X and Theory Y immediately become part of a purposive, either/or proposition just like the old managerial philosophy, because it is considered impossible for a manager to utilize both Theory X and Theory Y.

However, master managers do not create high performance by using one or the other of the philosophies described above; instead, they employ both. In this volume, I differentiate the purposive and the holistic philosophies or *frames*. As well, I define all the elements of both frames from a positive point of view, I demonstrate how an overemphasis on either one leads to negative consequences, and finally, I explain how the two frames are, in reality, inseparable. This insight tends to turn existing managerial theory upside down.

My first objective in writing *Beyond Rational Management* is to provide the practitioner with a conscious understanding of what he or she has felt intuitively about management. In this book I provide a variety of instruments and tools managers can use to develop a program for self-improvement. I also suggest ways for developing instructional programs based on the new concepts I advocate. I have discussed these ideas with U.S. business leaders in many seminars at the University of Michigan's executive program. Their response has been very positive. They quickly grasp the notions of competing values, tradeoffs, and paradox, for these describe their everyday experience.

My second objective in writing this book is to affect the thinking of scholars in the field of management and organization. The concepts contained in this book tend to be developmental and transformational, hence distant from many of the more mechanistic notions that currently dominate the field. I think, however, that the time has come for a more complex approach and, in Chapter One, I point out several current research programs that suggest that this is so.

Overview of the Contents

In Chapter One, I detail the practitioner's journey from novice to master manager. I explain how some managers learn to transcend their own style and assumptions about the nature of the world and develop the capacity to use multiple frames. Research findings on cognitive complexity, mastery, and ego development are reviewed briefly and linked to the argument that managers become increasingly effective as they develop a wider range of perspectives for viewing the world they live in.

Chapter Two explains how masters work with complexity and contradiction. Exploring the concepts of flow, peak experience, and excellence, this chapter demonstrates the dynamics of mastery. I clarify the transformational cycle and show how people move from the engagement of complexity and contradiction to creative insight and, then, to synergy, equilibrium, and mastery.

In Chapter Three, I discuss the barriers that frequently prevent practitioners from entering the transformational cycle and mastering management more readily. Alternative perspectives are introduced and exercises are presented to help the reader pinpoint his or her own strengths and weaknesses.

I explore the nature of competing values in modern organizations in Chapter Four. Drawing on a number of case examples, the chapter shows how organizations can be diagnosed from contradictory points of view. It shows how perspectives change over time and why some managerial careers are devastated by the practitioner's inability to understand such dynamics.

Chapter Five integrates the lessons of Chapters Three and Four and illustrates how our natural styles get us into trouble. I explain how the adherence to values that have yielded success in the past causes us to ignore positive values that are seemingly contradictory. This in turn leads to strategies that engage us in vicious cycles, which leave us no alternative but to get into greater difficulty. A dynamic theory of managerial effectiveness emerges from this discussion.

Building on the insights gained from Chapter Five, I present a model of managerial leadership in Chapter Six. This model, like the organizational model explored in Chapter Four, is based on a framework of competing perspectives. I outline the preferred roles and responsibilities of managers within each contradictory perspective and discuss the advantages and disadvantages of the framework.

In Chapter Seven, I review the results of an empirical study of effectiveness, which suggests that ineffective managers have great difficulty balancing competing philosophies and roles. They become trapped in their biases. Effective managers have a variety of styles. Although they may have one or two roles that are underplayed, their profiles are far more balanced than the profiles of ineffective managers. Master managers, on the other hand, are people who have transcended style.

Chapter Eight focuses on how managers can engage in the process of self-improvement. Although most major improvements in performance come from spontaneous transformations, it is also possible to make conscious steps toward mastery. The specific steps toward mastery are detailed and examples of each step are given.

In Chapter Nine, I provide instrumentation and other tools for executing the steps outlined in Chapter Eight. I supply a competing values instrument for self-analysis and for getting feedback from others, as well as other diagnostic materials.

Chapter Ten turns to the issues of skill building and education. I review a multimillion-dollar project in which the competing values model was operationalized in terms of skills and taught to several thousand managers. The strengths and weaknesses of this approach are also reviewed.

Acknowledgments

It has taken an enormously long time to write this relatively short book. Because the writing of the book has stretched over such a long period, there are many people whose assistance I should acknowledge. In doing so, I am sure that I will miss some people. Let me ask in advance for their forgiveness.

First, I would like to thank those people with whom I have coauthored publications over the past several years. In many instances in this volume I draw on coauthored papers in which key ideas were introduced. I am very grateful to David Andersen, Kim Cameron, Sue Faerman, Richard Hall, John Kimberly, Michael McGrath, John Rohrbaugh, and Michael Thompson. Each one has contributed valuably to the ideas in this book.

I am also grateful for the discussions, comments, or encouragements of colleagues such as Robert Backoff, Walter Balk, Bernard Bass, Warren Bennis, Wayne Brockbank, Jeffrey Ford, Donald Giek, Arie Lewin, David McCaffrey, Richard Mason, Phillip Mirvis, Max Sipporin, Thomas Taber, William Torbert, John Tropman, David Ulrich, Andrea Warfield, and Gary Yukl. As well, I would like to thank the many graduate students in Albany, New York, and Ann Arbor, Michigan, who have influenced my thinking.

I will always remember the efforts of the many staff members at the Institute for Government and Policy Studies; Rockefeller College, State University of New York, Albany; and the Graduate School of Business, University of Michigan–Ann Arbor, who spent long hours in preparing the manuscript. In particular, I would like to thank Marie Bien, Dianne Haft, Suzane Hagen, and Donna Noon. Finally, I must thank my wife, Delsa, and the children for their patience, understanding, and love.

Ann Arbor, Michigan   Robert E. Quinn
January 1988

The Author

Robert E. Quinn is professor of organizational behavior and human resource management at the Graduate School of Business, University of Michigan–Ann Arbor.

Quinn received his B.S. (1970) and M.S. (1971) degrees in sociology from Brigham Young University and his Ph.D. (1974) in organizational behavior and applied behavioral science from the University of Cincinnati. His main research activities have been in organizational and managerial effectiveness and in the management of change. He also continues to do research on the topics discussed in this volume. Quinn has published numerous journal articles as well as the following books: *Paradox and Transformation: Toward a Theory of Change in Organization and Management* (1988, with Kim S. Cameron), *New Futures: The Challenge of Managing Corporate Transitions* (1984, with John R. Kimberly), and *Organization Theory and Public Policy: Contributions and Limitations* (1983, with Richard H. Hall).

Beyond Rational Management

1

The Journey from Novice to Master Manager

As I listened to the man sitting in front of me, my mind ran backwards across the interviews that I had just completed. His subordinates and peers had given him glowing reviews: "Born to manage." "A great role model." "He is one person I am glad to work for."

As I tried to ask him questions that would unlock the mystery behind his success, an interesting story began to unfold. It seemed to involve both a crisis and a transformation.

After graduating from a five-year engineering program in four years, he had taken a job with his current organization. He had made a brilliant start and was promoted four times in eight years. He had the ability to take a complex technical problem and come up with a better answer than anyone else could. Initially he was seen as an innovative, action-oriented person with a bright future.

After his last promotion, however, everything started to change. He went through several very difficult years. For the first time he received serious negative feedback about his performance. His ideas and proposals were regularly rejected, and he was even passed over for a promotion. In reflecting on those days, he said:

> It was awful. Everything was always changing and nothing ever seemed to happen. The people above me would sit around forever and talk about things. The technically right answer didn't matter. They

1

were always making what I thought were wrong decisions, and when I insisted on doing what was right, they got pissed off and would ignore what I was saying. Everything was suddenly political. They would worry about what everyone was going to think about every issue. How you looked, attending cocktail parties—that stuff to me was unreal and unimportant.

I went through five and a half terrible years. I occasionally thought I had reached my level of incompetence, but I refused to give up. In the end, the frustration and pain turned out to be a positive thing because it forced me to consider some alternative perspectives. I eventually learned that there were other realities besides the technical reality.

I discovered perception and long time lines. At higher levels what matters is how people see the world, and everyone sees it a little differently. Technical facts are not as available or as important. Things are changing more rapidly at higher levels, you are no longer buffered from the outside world. Things are more complex, and it takes longer to get people on board. I decided I had to be a lot more receptive and a lot more patient. It was an enormous adjustment, but then things started to change. I think I became a heck of a lot better manager.

As a manager this man was not perfect. Clearly he had his share of bad days, and during the preceding year, a bad one for the industry, he had his share of defeats. There were occasions when he got discouraged and there were times when his subordinates felt he still acted too impulsively. Nevertheless, he had a wide range of capacities and most of the time displayed an ability to call upon them in successful ways. For the most part, he had become, with considerable effort, a master of management, a person with the capacity to create excellence.

The Concept of Mastery

If there is such a thing as a master of management, what is it that differentiates him or her from others? The answer has to do with how the master of management sees the world.

Most of us, like the engineer whom I interviewed, learn to think of the concept of organization in a very static way. Particularly at the lower levels, organizations seem to be characterized by relatively stable, predictable patterns of action. They appear to be, or at least we expect them to be, the product of rational-deductive thinking. We think of them as static mechanisms designed to accomplish some single purpose.

One of the most difficult things for most of us to understand is that organizations are dynamic. Particularly as one moves up the organizational ladder, matters become less tangible and less predictable. A primary characteristic of managing, particularly at higher levels, is the confrontation of change, ambiguity, and contradiction. Managers spend much of their time living in fields of perceived tensions. They are constantly forced to make trade-offs, and they often find that there are no right answers. The higher one goes in an organization, the more exaggerated this phenomenon becomes. One-dimensional bromides (care for people, work harder, get control, be innovative) are simply half-truths representing single domains of action. What exists in reality are contradictory pressures, emanating from a variety of domains. This fact is important because much of the time the choice is not between good and bad, but between one good and another or between two unpleasant alternatives. In such cases the need is for complex, intuitive decisions, and many people fail to cope successfully with the resulting tension, stress, and uncertainty. This is well illustrated by the initial failure and frustration of the engineer who was quoted earlier.

The people who come to be masters of management do not see their work environment only in structured, analytic ways. Instead, they also have the capacity to see it as a complex, dynamic system that is constantly evolving. In order to interact effectively with it, they employ a variety of different perspectives or frames. As one set of conditions arises, they focus on certain cues that lead them to apply a very analytic and structured approach. As these cues fade, they focus on new cues of emerging importance and apply another frame, perhaps this time an intuitive and flexible one. At another time they may emphasize the overall task, and at still another they may focus on the welfare of a single individual.

Because of these shifts, masters of management may appear to act in paradoxical ways. They engage the contradictions of organizational life by using paradoxical frames. Viewed from a single point in time, their behaviors may seem illogical and contradictory. Yet these seeming contradictions come together in a fluid whole. Things work out well for these people.

As illustrated in the case of the engineer, the ability to see the world in a dynamic fashion does not come naturally. It requires a dramatic change in outlook, a redefinition of one's world view. It means transcending the rules of mechanistic logic used for solving well-defined problems and adopting a more comprehensive and flexible kind of logic. It is a logic that comes from experience rather than from textbooks. It requires a change not unlike a religious conversion.

The capacity to master the contradictions of managerial life varies widely. There are the very, very few who excel and become masters. There are a few more who achieve a certain degree of mastery and do better than average. There are many in the middle of the continuum who are average. Finally, there are those who are ineffective but hang on and those who fail completely. In this book I will be concerned with each of these categories, but I will concentrate on those managers who succeed.

Because mastery is a paradoxical phenomenon, existing theories will not serve us very well. Most of these theories have a static bias. Here I will adopt a more dynamic point of view on management. Hence, in this book I will present some new concepts for thinking about the contradictory nature of management and organizational performance.

Mastery: Three Streams of Research

There is a growing literature on outstanding performance in the field of management. Here I will briefly review three streams of research. One has to do with thought processes of high-performing managers, another focuses on the movement from one developmental phase to another, and the last focuses on the evolution from novice to expert.

How Managers Think. Siegfried Streufert and his colleagues (Streufert and Swezey, 1986) have been involved in a number of empirical studies exploring what they call *cognitive complexity.* These researchers have found that cognitive complexity is associated with more moderated attitudes, openness to disconfirming information and adjustment in thinking, more effective discernment of the intents and strategies of others, better interrelationship of decisions, more appropriate strategy development, and more flexibility in consideration of distant goals. In general, they argue that highly complex individuals are more effective managers.

Cognitive complexity has to do with how people think about a domain or problem. The processes of differentiation and integration are crucial. Differentiation has to do with the use of bipolar scales such as short and tall, integration with the relationships among various dimensions. Complexity is the degree to which a domain is differentiated and integrated. The more dimensions and relationships that are used, the more cognitively complex a person is.

In thinking about football players, for example, we might use such dimensions as good-bad, weak-strong, active-passive, fast-slow. A person who uses all these dimensions would have a four-dimensional view of the world. Streufert and Swezey point out, however, that most of us are not so multidimensional about football. To test yourself, try to imagine a good, weak, passive, slow football player. If you cannot, it may be that you are really using the four dimensions as a single, collapsed dimension. That is, you may tend to employ good, strong, active, and fast in a nondifferentiated way. If a player has one characteristic, he must have them all. A football coach, in contrast, might use all the categories to differentiate. If so, he is more complex in his thinking about football players.

There are two kinds of integration, hierarchical and flexible. Hierarchical integrators see fixed relationships among dimensions and think that specific stimuli always affect the same dimensions in the same way. Flexible integrators see varied and changing relationships among dimensions. Hence, in operating in a given environment, they can be responsive to changes that require the reconceptualization of relationships. Hierarchical integrators function well in stable environments; flexible integrators function well in uncertain environments. A key question is whether or not flexible integrators can shift their style and perform as hierarchical integrators when necessary? Streufert and Swezey have preliminary evidence that suggests that this ability to shift is present in many but not all cognitively complex managers. This issue is important because it implies an evolutionary process as depicted in the next two streams of research.

Torbert's Developmental Model. The second stream of work takes an evolutionary perspective. Torbert (1987) has applied the psychological theories of ego development to the field of management. He argues that there are seven stages to this development and that the evolution from one stage to another requires a restructuring or transition in one's philosophy or world view. At each higher level, the individual continues to have the capacities of the lower levels. Managers appear in stages 3, 4, 5, and 6, and so I will briefly review these four levels.

Stage 3 is called the diplomat stage. While this stage is commonly associated with teen-agers, some managers, particularly at lower levels, are also found here. They are able to appreciate the preferences of others; in fact, conformity to group norms is one of their central concerns. Loyalty and harmony are important, while public conflict and the loss of face are the greatest evils.

In their late teen years people often make the transition from the diplomat to the technician (fourth) stage. Here they identify with an external system that has high internal logic or order. This might have to do with car engines, computer programs, the scientific method, mathematics, or a well-defined bureaucracy. For managers this means an identification with expertise. The manager's role is to know everything. He or she must understand the subordinate's job better than the subordinate understands it. This kind of manager is consumed with details and demands perfection. Torbert cites data showing that the largest number of managers fall into this category.

In the fifth or achiever stage people take on an identity of their own. They are less reactive and less given to making excuses. They become more goal oriented and take more responsibility for their behavior. Here people are open to feedback and will adjust their behavior in order to achieve their goals. They are not married to a single point of view. They become more at home in a variety of domains. Instead of concentrating on technical questions, they come to appreciate the importance of interpersonal relations, marketing, politics, and so on. They take on a higher level of cognitive complexity. "Such managers are committed to achieving results in a complex real world characterized by the collision of many types of logic, many scales of social system, and many different temporal rhythms" (Torbert, 1987, p. 111). The second largest proportion of managers falls into this category.

The strategist is the sixth stage of development. It was reached by only 14 percent of the managers studied, and these were all at the senior management level. The thinking process of these people is highly complex. They "delight in paradoxes and anomalies," they "respond flexibly to the historical process as it generates events" (Torbert, 1987, p. 143). They are not totally focused on goals. They develop a capacity to generate new orders or organizations. In particular, the strategist realizes that all frames through which the world is seen are relative. No one frame is better than another. This discovery particularly qualifies the strategist to understand the uniqueness of each individual and situation.

According to Torbert, of particular importance at the higher level of development is action inquiry, that is, the capacity to explore a developing situation while acting on the priority of highest apparent importance and, if appropriate, simultaneously inviting a reframing or restructuring. The difference between action inquiry and normal thought processes is that action and inquiry are woven together in one fluid process. They are not kept separate.

Flexible integration and action inquiry represent similar concepts. The developmental perspective suggests that people who have acquired this capacity also retain the capacity to function in more routinized situations. The last stream of research suggests a similar conclusion.

Evolution of Mastery. Some researchers have been able to track the evolutionary development of expertise or mastery in different fields of activity. Dreyfus, Dreyfus, and Athanasion (1986) have reviewed this work and have provided a five-stage model that describes the evolution from novice to expert.

In the novice stage people learn facts and rules. The rules are learned as absolutes that are never to be violated. For example, in playing chess people learn the names of the pieces, how they are moved, and their value. They are told to exchange pieces of lower value for pieces of higher value. In management, this might be the equivalent of the classroom education of an M.B.A.

In the advanced beginner stage, experience becomes critical. Performance improves somewhat as real situations are encountered. Understanding begins to exceed the stated facts and rules. Observation of certain basic patterns leads to the recognition of factors that were not set forth in the rules. A chess player, for example, begins to recognize certain basic board positions that should be pursued. The M.B.A. discovers the basic norms, values, and culture of the workplace on the first job.

The third stage is competence. Here the individual has begun to appreciate the complexity of the task and now recognizes a much larger set of cues. The person develops the ability to select and concentrate on the most important cues. With this ability competence grows. Here the reliance on absolute rules begins to disappear. People take calculated risks and engage in complex trade-offs. A chess player may, for example, weaken board position in order to attack the opposing king. This plan may or may not follow any rules that the person was ever taught. The M.B.A. may go beyond the technical analysis taught in graduate school as he or she experiments with an innovation of some sort. Flow or excellence may even be experienced in certain specific domains or subareas of management, as in the case of the engineer at the beginning of the chapter who displayed technical brilliance.

In the proficiency stage, calculation and rational analysis seem to disappear, and unconscious, fluid, and effortless performance begins to emerge. Here no one plan is held sacred. The person learns to unconsciously "read" the evolving situation. Cues are noticed and responded to, and attention shifts to new cues as the importance of the old ones recedes. New plans are triggered as emerging patterns call to mind plans that worked previously. Here there is a holistic and intuitive grasp of the situation. Here we are talking, for example, about the top 1 percent of all chess players, the people with the ability to intuitively recognize and respond to change in board positions. Here the M.B.A. has become an effective, upper-level manager, capable of meeting a wide variety of demands and contradictions.

Experts, those at the fifth stage, do what comes naturally. They do not apply rules but use holistic recognition in a way that allows them to deeply understand the situation. They have maps of the territory programmed into their heads that the rest of us are not aware of. They see and know things intuitively that the rest of us do not know or see (many dimensions). They frame and reframe strategies as they read changing cues (action inquiry). Here the manager has fully transcended personal style. The master manager seems to effortlessly meet the contradictions of organizational life.

Here, again, we see a similarity to flexible integration and action inquiry. Each of these three streams of research suggests a kind of thinking that is complex, holistic, and fluid—a kind of thinking that distinguishes the master from the novice.

An Illustration

The ability to enter a complex action setting and to see it from more than one perspective, indeed, to see it from contrasting perspectives, is not easy. It is for this reason that the novice has difficulty in even conceiving of management from a complex and dynamic perspective. Perhaps a very simple story will help to illustrate the point.

On one occasion in my introductory M.B.A. class the topic was groups, and the students were asked to engage in several group activities. I then gave a lecture on the topic. I began by pointing out that groups evolve through predictable stages and that if this evolutionary process is managed correctly, the group can become one of the manager's most powerful tools. In "turned on" groups people get inspired and work productively without much need for intervention or control on the part of the boss. After presenting several concrete examples, I then pointed out that few managers ever experience this phenomenon because they destroy the evolutionary process in its early stages. I presented a list of task functions and a list of process functions that must occur in order for a group to evolve. As we discussed such task functions as initiating structure, giving information, clarifying, summarizing, and evaluating, the students had little difficulty. But when we turned to functions such as process observation, empathy, participation, surfacing rather than smothering conflict, and managing interpersonal tension in positive ways, they seemed more challenged.

After class, one of the students wanted to talk. He said he had noticed that when his group first met, one of the members did not take part in the discussion. After the first meeting he decided that he would try to include the student. But, he told me, "I totally failed. When you assigned the second exercise, I noticed that this guy was again sitting around and not saying anything. But I decided that I could not do anything about it. We had only so much time and the work had to get done. I do not think it is possible to get the work done and also do those other things you were talking about. You cannot think about both things at the same time."

In this case the student was perfectly illustrating the difference between the way a novice thinks and the way a master thinks. With this particular contradiction, the novice applies one perspective, usually justified by the rhetoric of purpose or goal achievement, and stays with it, never discovering that he or she, from a larger perspective, is destroying the productivity being sought in the first place. The master, reading cues from the situation, calls on both a task view and a process view. Two contrasting domains are understood and woven together. The result is a much higher level of productivity—a level that many managers never experience.

2

Achieving High Performance:
A Paradoxical View
of Excellence

The journey from novice to master is a long and difficult one. In sports, art, or work, a master knows and understands the many elements of an action domain and sees things in the domain that the novice does not see. The master responds to the cues that he or she encounters in complex, creative ways that reflect a deep, internalized theory. The results are oneness with the task and fluidity of performance. Hidden beneath this surface manifestation of mastery, however, is a capacity to continuously hold, test, and experiment with opposing conceptualizations of reality. The novice, limited by the mechanistic assumptions that are implanted by technical instruction, has little understanding of such a notion.

The mastery of management is linked to the capacity to create excellence. Like Pirsig's (1974) notion of quality in *Zen and the Art of Motorcycle Maintenance*, excellence is a concept that has not been easy for the Western mind to grasp. Excellence is a paradoxical phenomenon that emerges under conditions of uncertainty and creative tension. It is also an idiosyncratic and dynamic phenomenon. Paradoxical, uncertain, creative, and idiosyncratic behaviors do not readily lend themselves to the mechanistic assumptions of Western thought. In order to understand the concept of mastery, we need new theories (Van de Ven, 1983) and new methods (Streufert and Swezey, 1986). In this chapter I will begin our exploration of mastery by presenting a new perspective on excellence. I will suggest that it is a dynamic phenomenon that can be thought of as a peak experience. I will then present a model of how excellence occurs. Next, I will consider the implications of the model and provide a description of the master manager as someone who can transcend technique and engage the world in more effective ways.

Excellence as Peak Performance

When individuals experience excellence or peak performance, they often describe this experience by using phrases such as "I was really on," "I was in the groove," "I was on a roll," or "I was really high." Such statements are an overall reflection of a process that Csikszentmihalyi (1975) calls "flow." In his study of peak experiences, he viewed a wide variety of activities and concluded that when people experience flow they are completely involved in what they are doing. The level and intensity of challenge leave no time for boredom. Their skills are fully employed, and their actions have real and predictable consequences that are clearly fed back to the actors. During this dynamic state of total involvement there is a holistic sensation that suggests a lack of conscious intervention by the actor. While one knows how one is doing, because of the feedback, there is no stopping for conscious evaluation. Questions such as How well am I doing? interrupt the process. In this state of flow, according to Csikszentmihalyi, there is no split between the self and the environment, the stimulus and the response, the past and the present. Action and awareness are merged. There are no dualisms. The self disappears.

While the experience of peak performance is frequently associated with play, creative activity, and religious experiences, it also occurs in various work settings. Surgeons often experience it in the operating room as do aviators in flight. Tasks such as writing a report or making a presentation also provide opportunities for experiencing flow. Kriegel and Kriegel (1984), for example, report the experience of a marketing manager who had to make her first presentation to her company's vice-president of finance. She was worried because she knew him to be a "by the numbers" person and her presentation contained some controversial and conjectural points. Her worry increased when she found out that the president of the company was also going to be at the presentation. When she started talking, however, she was surprised to find that she felt calm and unintimidated. She seemed to anticipate the president's and vice-president's concerns and had the perfect answer for all their questions. The two officers were deeply impressed with her presentation and gave her all the resources that she needed. She later marveled at her level of performance and the feeling of exhilaration associated with the experience.

The phenomenon is not limited to individuals acting alone. Dee Hock, the former CEO at Visa International, describes the phenomenon as follows: "In the field of group endeavor, you will see incredible events in which the group performs far beyond the sum of its individual talents. It happens in the symphony, in the ballet, in the theater, in sports, and equally in business. It is easy to recognize and impossible to define. It is a mystique. It cannot be achieved without immense effort, training, and cooperation, but effort, training, and cooperation alone rarely create it. Some groups reach it consistently. Few can sustain it" (Schlesinger, Eccles, and Gabarro, 1983, p. 486). The interface of big dreams, hard work, and successful outcomes is potent. The sensation that accompanies the phenomenon is a feeling of exhilaration.

Bill Russell, former center of the world-champion Boston Celtics, calls this feeling of exhilaration "magic" and provides another example at the collective level. Occasionally a Celtic game would "heat up" to the point that it would become "more than a physical or even mental" experience. Play would rise to an extraordinary level. Something would surround not only the Celtics but the other team and the referees as well. Usually it would happen when the Celtics were playing a better-than-average team. It would start with three or four of the best players on each team making outstanding plays. Then a special feeling would spread across both teams. Each person on the floor would push himself harder and harder. Russell goes on:

> At that special level all sorts of odd things happened. The game would be in a white heat of com-

petition, and yet somehow I wouldn't feel competitive — which is a miracle in itself. I'd be putting out the maximum effort, straining, and yet nothing could surprise me. It was almost as if we were playing in slow motion. During those spells I could almost sense how the next play would develop and where the next shot would be taken. Even before the other team brought the ball in bounds, I could feel it so keenly that I'd want to shout to my teammates, "It's coming there!" — except that I knew everything would change if I did. My premonitions would be consistently correct, and I always felt then that I not only knew all the Celtics by heart but also all the opposing players, and that they all knew me. There have been many times in my career when I felt moved or joyful, but these were the moments when I had chills pulsing up and down my spine [Russell and Brauch, 1979, p. 177].

Russell uses paradoxical statements to portray this unusual event. It is a process that transcends its physical (objective) and mental (subjective) elements, one that is competitive but not competitive, one that is excruciatingly painful but without pain, one filled with surprise that surprises no one, an intense but delicate process that can be brought to a halt by the simplest mistake by any player on the floor. This experience of paradox and transcendence is often associated with peak experiences. In order to comprehend it more fully, we will consider it within a dynamic context.

Transformational Cycle: The Individual Level

I conceive of excellence or peak experience as something that temporarily emerges as part of a dynamic cycle. The cycle is called the transformational cycle not only because it has a transformational phase, during which excellence occurs, but because it has a number of changing phases that represent very different conditions. To stay within the cycle, a person or group must continually change.

In the lower-right-hand corner of Figure 1 is the initiation phase of the transformational cycle. The cycle begins when, for whatever reason, a person or group desires to improve and begins to take risks. At this point it is very common to receive feedback that disconfirms the strategy behind the risk-taking step. This can lead one out of the cycle and into a state of panic. But one can also continue to engage the disconfirmation, thereby fully entering the uncertainty phase and there engaging in intense, intuitive experimentation. If these action experiments continue to fail, the process can once again lead the individual out of the cycle and into a state of panic. But if, instead, the individual is able to tolerate contradiction, he or she may be able to gain a creative insight that leads to the transformational phase. That is, through intuitive, experimental learning, the contradictory elements may be put together or "reframed" as a new theory or paradigm emerges. This new vision integrates the previously contradictory elements and results in synergy. It is here that excellence or peak performance occurs. Great energy is released as the person enters a Zen-like state and, like the marketing manager, Dee Hock, or Bill Russell, becomes one with the task. In this phase a person can again leave the cycle by entering a state of exhaustion. In contrast, the new understanding can be routinized as the relationships move into a more stable equilibrium and the task is more fully mastered. Here stagnation provides an alternative to continuing the cycle. On the pages that follow I will elaborate and more fully explain the cycle.

Initiation Phase. In the initiation phase, for any of a wide number of reasons, a person has a desire to change. There is a need to do something that he or she is not absolutely sure about. On the one hand, this desire may lead the person to take some risks and engage in a new pattern of action. On the other hand, the person might have a strong fear of failure and decide not to engage in the new behavior. If that happens, the cycle will be broken and the individual will begin or continue to stagnate. To fuel the cycle in the initiation phase, an individual must exercise faith (not a popular topic in social science but perhaps one that

Figure 1. The Transformational Cycle.

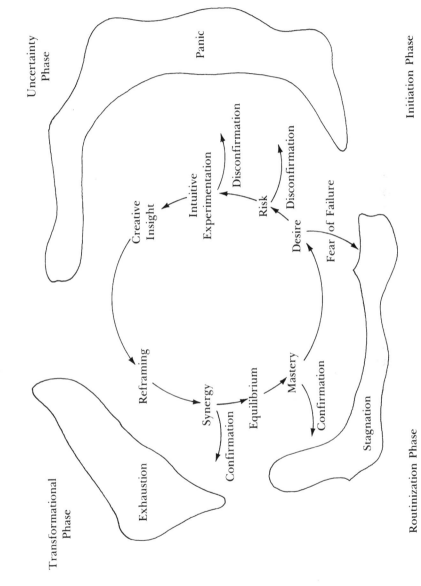

should receive more attention) and engage in the new action patterns.

Because the cycle requires a leap of faith, it is not surprising that studies of high performers often note the presence of a positive outlook and an unusual perspective on failure. For example, after interviewing many high performers, including a number of successful executives, Bennis and Nanus (1985) noted that these high performers prefer not to use the word *failure* but instead use words such as *false start, glitch, mess,* or *error.* These people see failure as something that is acceptable and not to be dreaded. It is part of a learning process necessary to growth, not a final outcome to be avoided at all costs. High performers combined vision, persistence, consistency, and self-confidence. For them, failure was a stepping-stone.

This attitude toward failure is not confined to excellence in management. It is interesting to note that even in science the principle seems to hold (Daft, 1983). Researchers, for example, are taught in graduate school that science is a "by the book" process. Rigor, control, planning, and the removal of all uncertainties are critical. Like managers, however, they soon learn that this "tight," textbook approach does not fit the real world. If this approach truly fits the problem, it is likely that the problem and the eventual analytic answer will not be very interesting. Rigor is traded for significance. The literature suggests that tolerance of uncertainty and failure plays a key role in outstanding research (Thomas, 1974). Landmark studies usually turn out to be "loosely done" (Daft and Wiginton, 1979; Mackenzie and House, 1978). They also tend to result from contact with real world problems and open-ended questions (Lundberg, 1976).

It appears that in all areas of activity, if one is to progress, one must be willing to take risks. Contrary to much rational-technical thinking, the initiation of action under conditions of risk is an important step in pursuing high performance. It is here that a master manager begins to move beyond technique.

Uncertainty Phase. Once the new action pattern is engaged, it creates a reaction. A young girl, for example, may attempt her first unassisted ride on a bicycle. Someone gives her a push across the driveway. Her attention is intensely focused as she tries to keep the bicycle upright. After a moment, however, the feedback loop sets in. If her experimental strategy for engaging the task is not working, the bike begins to tilt and she sees the earth rapidly coming closer. She experiences panic as she falls. But if she overcomes her feeling of panic and keeps pedaling, the bike stays up and she finds herself moving forward across the yard. Here she is in a state of high uncertainty. She teeters between success and failure. Here learning is highly intuitive. The key for the young girl is not to panic but to continue under uncertainty, and with each push of the pedal and turn of the handlebars to improve her experimental strategy.

Living with opposition and tolerating uncertainty and contradictions were found to be crucial elements in a forty-year study of the lives of Harvard graduates (Vaillant, 1977). The subjects in Vaillant's study were a cohort of men who had graduated in the early 1940s. Selected because of their positive qualifications, most distinguished themselves as officers during the Second World War and then went on to occupy important professional positions of various sorts. In the course of their lives all these men experienced opposition. What concerned Vaillant was how they coped with their problems, hence the title of his study, *Adaptation to Life*. One finding was that some people employed healthy mechanisms to cope with life's problems while others employed maladaptive mechanisms. Of two men who each experienced a disintegrating romantic relationship, one might cope with the pain of a broken heart by committing suicide, the other by writing great poetry. Vaillant suggests that the more healthy men met opposition with creative, caring, and productive strategies while the less healthy used strategies that were neither productive nor caring.

It seems that the tolerance of ambiguity and the engagement of contradiction are crucial in learning through intuitive experimentation. This tends to be confirmed by Bartunek, Gordon, and Weathersby (1983), who reviewed the discussion of literature on complex thinking processes in Chapter One of this volume and concluded that highly uncertain situations require cognitive complexity (also see Streufert and Swezey, 1986). This includes both differentiation, (the ability to perceive several different dimensions in a stimulus array) and integration (the ability to develop complex connections among differentiated characteristics). People who are cognitively complex can use more than one frame to make sense of the world. According to Bartunek, Gordon, and Weathersby, the literature indicates that this ability correlates with tolerance for ambiguity, assumption of leadership, prediction accuracy, empathy, and conflict resolution. It is crucial to creative insight and the process of reframing, a central element in the next phase and a primary capacity of the master manager.

Transformational Phase. Because creative insight and reframing are so tightly linked, it is difficult to differentiate between the uncertainty phase and the transformational phase. Reframing almost instantaneously follows creative insight.

Reframing means moving to a different kind of comprehension. It is the emergence of a new view or theory that suddenly makes sense of a contradictory situation. Kuhn (1970) spoke of such changes in science as scientific revolutions. But the ability to transcend or reframe perceptual tensions is at the heart of change in all fields of endeavor. This fact is well illustrated in the work of Rothenberg (1979), who introduced the term *Janusian thinking* while investigating the creative breakthroughs of Mozart, Picasso, Einstein, and fifty-five other highly creative people. Janusian thinking was found to be the common thought pattern explaining all the breakthroughs and important contributions made by these individuals. Their innovations occurred when opposites were brought together. Contrary to existing logic, the creative person saw the integrated functioning of antithetical elements. Einstein, for example, noted that a falling object could be at rest in relation to another falling object, while not at rest in relation to the point from which it was falling. From this paradoxical observation came the theory of relativity that eventually transformed all of modern life. Rothenberg's study of other creative breakthroughs tended to show the same pattern.

Hampden-Turner (1981) had a notion similar to Janusian

thinking in mind when he observed that a paradox may simply be the failure to comprehend "recursive systems which operate in patterns of mutual restraint and coordination" (p. 112). Hence, the creative individual "flirts with doubt and disorder, enduring anxiety while intuiting the answer to his doubts" (p. 112). From this process an embryonic solution emerges and initiates a reordering process, or a reframing. This is the shift from uncertainty to the transformational phase.

The reframing process results in a synergistic integration. Here the observer and the observed, the actor and the action become one. Because of the reframing process the observer can "see." It is like a religious conversion. The new theory allows for a new, more intense relationship between the observer and the observed, between the actor and that which is acted upon. The object becomes an object of passion (Maslow, 1962). Knowing it in this new way brings marvelous stimulation. The action becomes a labor of love. The observer and the object, the actor and the action now form a reinforcing system.

A somewhat common observation in writings on this subject is that the process involves a trance-like state in which great mental focus is present. The person becomes totally involved in the task. For example, John Brodie, an all-pro quarterback, has noted, as Bill Russell did earlier, that there is "no past or future" during such experiences, and that time slows down as if everything were in slow motion. According to Brodie, "It seems as if I have all the time in the world to watch the receivers run their patterns, and yet I know the defensive line is coming at me as fast as ever. I know perfectly well how hard and fast those guys are coming, and yet the whole thing seems like a movie or a dance in slow motion" (Kriegel and Kriegel, 1984, p. 97).

The intense mental focus achieved during this kind of flow is seemingly related to the fusion or oneness that occurs. The person and the task are not two separate, distant things. Instead, they have a spontaneous and harmonious relationship in which they become a mutually reinforcing system.

It is here in the cycle that excellence occurs. It is here that people reach new heights. In some cases the action might involve a truly unique accomplishment such as achieving a new

Olympic record. At other times the accomplishment is unique to the participant. The little girl, for example, rides across the lawn with a feeling of exhilaration, or the marketing executive gets on a "roll" as she makes a spectacular presentation. In each case magic occurs. The audience, whether the helping parent, the critical boss, or the fans in the Olympic stadium, also become part of the process. They are caught by the "contagion," they feel the "magic." It is the presence or absence of this contagion that accounts for the standing ovation at one event and the passive applause at another. Vaillant (1977), for example, noted that high performers have a positive, inspirational impact on others. Their enthusiasm spreads.

Excellence does not last forever. As exhilarating as it is, it does require full extension of the human system. It can be broken by an external interruption, such as a referee's whistle, or by internal depletion of energy. Indeed, after a peak experience people often report absolute exhaustion.

Routinization Phase. Once a person has experienced flow or high performance, the phenomenon becomes a little less awesome. The little girl "has the hang of it." She "knows" how to ride. She begins to acquire more specific control over the process. Now when she goes out and picks up the bicycle, she feels little sense of risk. Riding across the lawn has become less exciting. Her new theory, which came with reframing, fully explains what is happening. The process is understood, and all seeming contradictions have disappeared. At this point deductive thought processes begin to prove useful. The primary process is logical and critical and simply involves error correction. If the bike is leaning to one side, the rider simply adjusts the handlebars and leans slightly to the other side. Here the clearly understood relationships make logical action appropriate. For example, if the temperature goes down, a person puts on more clothes; if it goes up, the person takes off some clothes. This is what Argyris (1976) calls "single-loop learning."

In the basketball example provided by Bill Russell, the high level of performance simply cannot be sustained indefinitely. The players would collapse in exhaustion. Hence, moments of peak performance are followed by periods of equilibrium in which the players perform in a more routine way. In the case of the marketing executive the same principle holds. She simply could not maintain the same level of intensity for an indefinite period of time.

In the routinization phase, complex, creative thought processes are not necessary. A mechanistic world view of clear cause-and-effect relationships is distilled from the experiences in the last two phases. So valued is the new theory that when events do not fit, the events are often reinterpreted rather than the theory. The danger here is that what was competence at one point may lead to incompetence at some other point. It is also possible to strive to avoid all situations where the theory does not fit. This strategy leads to stagnation and again moves one out of the cycle.

The Problem with Excellence

The notion of excellence or peak performance is a very exciting concept and has been the subject of much interest in recent years. Excellence, however, is not a fixed state that can be created by following a recipe. You have to be lucky. After doing your best, you may still fail to create excellence. If the external conditions are not right, it simply will not happen. Excellence is also a very fragile phenomenon. It is easily shattered. Even though you are doing everything extraordinarily well, you may totally fail because of a negative turn in some key external factor.

While excellence is difficult to create and difficult to maintain in the short run, perhaps its most important characteristic is that it cannot be maintained over a long period of time. By its very nature, excellence is a temporary phenomenon. It cannot be maintained indefinitely. The transformational stage will inevitably be followed by the routinization stage.

A New Kind of Theory

The above insight turns the traditional logic of management theory upside down. A dynamic theory emerges. It suggests that while at some points it is appropriate to rationally pursue excellence, the next step may be to leave rationality and control behind. The master manager must be willing to engage risk and trust intuition. At another point, when excellence exists, the appropriate thing to do is to begin trying to understand it and routinize what has been gained. Here the challenge is to leave behind intuition and exhilaration and move toward control and rationality. At this point, one pursues excellence by walking away from it.

The assumptions of current management theory are static. If we look through the lenses of tradition, the seeming contradictions in the theory being set forth here are almost incomprehensible. If we look through the lenses of a dynamic model, however, the contradictions disappear. We see for the first time the oppositions that simultaneously exist in the world of management. We recognize that those ideologies that advocate a particular set of values as the necessary basis of good management can become rhetorical blinders. There is no one right answer in a dynamic world. Ultimately the mastery of management, particularly as one moves up the system, hinges neither on intuition nor on rationality alone but on the constant movement between the two.

The key to becoming a master manager is seeing past one's own blinders and the blinders imposed by the expectations of others. You begin to do this by obtaining an awareness of your own style, learning what your own strengths and blind spots are. You must then make a conscious effort to appreciate the importance of your weaknesses. What is it that you tend not to see? What skills do you tend to ignore? This kind of thinking is not easy. It involves a certain amount of cognitive complexity and means experimenting with opposing frames of reference. It does not come by reading. Like the little girl learning to ride a bike, you have to throw yourself into the process and learn by experience.

3

Mastering the Contradictions
of Organizational Life

In the last chapter I discussed the particular state of high performance that is implied by words such as *flow, peak experience,* and *excellence.* I suggested that in order to enter this state a person must use the dynamic perspectives of the master rather than the static perspectives of the novice. Often, the contrast between these two viewpoints is great. For example, consider the following description.

"Sometime look at a novice workman or a bad workman and compare his expression with that of a craftsman whose work you know is excellent and you'll see the difference. The craftsman isn't ever following a single line of instruction. He's making decisions as he goes along. For that reason he'll be absorbed and attentive to what he's doing even though he doesn't deliberately contrive this. His motions and the machine are in a kind of harmony. He isn't following any set of written instructions because the nature of the material at hand determines his thoughts and motions, which simultaneously change the nature of the material at hand. The material and his thoughts are changing together in a progression of changes until his mind's at rest at the same time the material's right" (Pirsig, 1974, p. 148).

There is a marked difference between the novice and the master. The novice does not understand the transformational cycle, but is limited by reliance on deductive rules, fear of failure, and hesitancy to engage risk and uncertainty. In contrast, the master moves confidently through the cycle, each time achieving a greater understanding of the unknown, a fuller appreciation of excellence and how to create it. Thus the master gains a complex, holistic, and paradoxical understanding of the cycle. This is a complex process that tends to defy abstraction and articulation. Most people call it intuition and treat it as though it were a mystery. Actually it is very much dependent on rules, discipline, and structure, but these are veiled and seem to disappear for a time. This paradoxical process allows the master to engage a task in a coevolutionary way. Both the object and the master change. They reinforce each other in a transformational process.

The master has an internalized, complex theory that the novice does not have. The process of reading changing cues and employing contrasting frames is not easy. In order to comprehend why, it is important to understand three things: how we become blinded by our purposes, the role of information processing in this blinding, and the relationship between information processing and how we think about organizing and managing.

How We Become Blinded by Our Purposes

Thinking about contradiction is not a natural inclination. It requires counterintuitive processes. The natural tendency for people socialized around Western thought is to be what Bateson (1979) calls "schismogenic." The term *schismogenesis* ("creation of schisms") refers to arguments, theories, or perspectives that are broken or split (*schismo*) at the outset (*genesis*). One of two opposing but connected values is chosen over another. When a person seeks to pursue a goal or to explain or make sense of a phenomenon (a conscious purpose), a logical (internally consistent) set of abstractions is constructed. This kind of thinking defines away contradiction and eliminates paradoxes. While this kind of thinking is useful in pursuing a goal, it also produces a unidimensional mental set that tends to be blind to emerging cues that require another perspective.

When behaving with a conscious purpose, people tend to act upon the environment, not with it. They seek to impose their wills. Again, this is a useful way of acting, but the assumption, paradigm, or world view that underlies such rational-deductive

approaches prevents us from seeing or appreciating the recursive nature of the world or the feedback loops that connect us to
the environment we are altering. Contradictions must be cir-
cumvented or crushed. Adaptation and transformation are
made difficult. Since we all act with conscious purposes, we are
all, whether management theorists, practicing managers, or
laypersons, experienced in schismogenesis. Perhaps an example
for each group will be useful.

Theorists. In their popular book, *In Search of Excellence*, Peters
and Waterman (1982) seek to discover what differentiates excellent companies from ordinary ones. Embedded in their work is
an observation that is quite consistent with our observations up
to this point. They conclude that managers in excellent companies have an unusual ability to resolve paradox, to translate
conflicts and tensions into excitement, high commitment, and
superior performance. In reviewing the book, Van de Ven (1983)
applauds this insight and notes a grave inadequacy in the theories generated by administrative researchers. He argues that
while the managers of excellent companies seem to have a
capacity for dealing with paradox, administrative theories are
not designed to take this phenomenon into account. In order to
be internally consistent, theorists tend to eliminate contradiction. Hence, there is a need for a dynamic theory that can handle
both stability and change, that can consider the tensions and
conflicts inherent in human systems. Among other things, the
theory would view people as complex actors in tension-filled
social systems, constantly interacting with a "fast-paced, ever-
changing array of forces" (Van de Ven, 1983, p. 624). The theory
would center on transforming leadership that focuses on "the
ethics and value judgments that are implied when leaders and
followers raise one another to higher levels of motivation and
morality" (p. 624).

The empirical foundations of traditional social science
stand in the way of attempts to build such a theory. Empiricism
is primarily a rational-deductive perspective designed to answer
the question, What is? It is constantly breaking things apart,
looking for linear, cause-and-effect relationships. These are al-

most always sought after with a purposefulness that results in a schismogenic view, which is often quite distinct from the outlook of the next researcher. This helps to account for some of the confusion that characterizes the literature on managerial effectiveness.

Managers. The need for internally consistent logic may also be a problem for managers. Typically, coalitions with certain common interests confront the major uncertainties facing an organization. They hold the power and control the policies that are often initially successful. However, over time, the policies may cease to work. A crisis occurs, and a new coalition comes to control the organization's power, resources, and policy making. Hence, at one point the dominant coalition may be comprised of people from production, at another time it may be made up of people with a marketing, legal, or financial background.

Later in the book I will examine an expanding firm whose successful growth strategy became a source of difficulties. Top management's simultaneous emphasis on productivity and collective decision making resulted, as planned, in growth, but it also increased the workload of executives. This increased workload led to a loss of cohesion. The company found that it needed to decrease emphasis on productivity and to increase emphasis on maintenance functions such as training and internal coordination. However, such a decision was contrary to the prevailing logic that productivity brings growth. Top management could not make the seemingly obvious change in strategy. As a result, conflict continued to increase until key people in the top management group were replaced. The rigidity of their beliefs prevented them from perceiving and creatively engaging the contradictions in their environment.

Laypersons. Another example of schismogenesis is provided by Hampden-Turner (1981) in his description of how hawks and doves perceived each other during the Vietnam War. Hawks saw themselves as oriented to patriotism, authority, and loyalty, while doves described hawks as being oriented to militarism, elitism, and conformity. Doves saw themselves as favoring dissent, equality, and rebellion, while hawks saw doves as subversive and disloyal.

Note that it is in the language used that the split occurs. The potentially manageable conservative-liberal difference is transformed into an unmanageable difference between good and evil. Because of the wholly positive-negative structure of the language, each side becomes wedded to what it sees as the only moral alternative. As Hampden-Turner points out, this condition results in several problems. Because there can be no agreement on premises, and because each party feels threatened by the other and cannot see itself as the other sees it, there can be no real engagement and communication. Both parties must remain blind to the view of the other. Because of the closed nature of each set of ideas, each party becomes increasingly aware that its own theory is faulty in tracking and explaining what is in reality happening. Both sides become increasingly threatened by the failure of their moral maps to predict "realities." This frustration often leads to the need to "celebrate the map itself," that is, to make the idea sacred while denying the reality. Feedback, learning, adaptation, and transformation are all precluded.

Schismogenic thinking, then, is purposeful thinking, which often includes implicit value judgments that split off competing positive values. These undesired positive values are pushed away, separated, lost to consideration. Reality is distorted. Dogmatic strategies are pursued while the negatively defined lost complement gathers energy and grows in its subterranean hiding place, ever distorting the contours of the strategic landscape. Soon the dogged pursuit of a given strategy brings unanticipated consequences or, in some cases, major catastrophes.

Before going on, let us again note that purposeful thinking is not inherently inappropriate or wrong. Indeed, it is necessary and useful. The problem is simply that purposive thinking often discourages us from seeing certain cues and employing contradictory frames. It oversimplifies and distorts reality.

Role of Information Processing in the Blinding Process

Of the many problems that contribute to the blinding process and prevent us from seeing and understanding dynamic patterns, one of the most important is the way we prefer to process information. Our values, motives, and problem-solving styles all tend to reflect certain information-processing perspectives. These help us to see certain things and blind us to others. In order to illustrate this point, I will employ three very simple exercises — one on values, a second on motives, and a third on problem solving. (Note that these are short, illustrative exercises written for this chapter and are not meant to be used for research purposes.)

Values. The first exercise asks you to consider the following eight pairs of proverbs. Circle the one in each pair that you feel is more correct.

1a. Ultimately there is but one truth.

1b. There are two sides to every story.

2a. Nothing is so meaningful as a job well done.

2b. Greatest meaning derives from loving relationships.

3a. Custom deters progress.

3b. Wisdom favors tradition.

4a. The only constant is change.

4b. Order follows regulation.

5a. Establish the rule and allow no variation.

5b. Be tolerant, for each rule has its exception.

6a. Never do less than your individual best.

6b. Seek understanding, for it brings cooperation.

7a. Be wise as a serpent and gentle as a dove.

7b. Act aggressively or the moment will be lost.

8a. Dream well for thy dreams shall be prophets.

8b. Do well the little things that lie nearest.

You might like to stop and circle the proverb in each pair that you think is most correct. Many people find this to be a difficult task. Proverbs such as these are often taken as givens, as unquestioned statements of what the world is like. When a proverb is juxtaposed with a contrasting one, however, the observer experiences some contradiction. It soon becomes clear

that such statements represent more a matter of value preference than a matter of absolute truth.

The first four sets of proverbs are contrasting statements
about the nature of the world. The second four sets are statements of behavioral strategy — ways in which one should operate
in order to be successful in the world. In Figure 2 we array these
eight sets as a framework. The statements are at the ends of the
inner axis while the strategies are around the outer edge. As we
contrast the values in one part of the diagram with an opposite
area, we can begin to understand the importance of values and
assumptions in determining how people tend to see and behave.
You should circle the statements in Figure 2 that you circled in
the list of contrasting values.

Motives. Let us now turn to a second exercise. This exercise
focuses on motives and what you would like to achieve through
your work. Listed below are eight sets of characteristics that
might describe a work situation. In an ideal work situation, how
frequently should each of the following characteristics be emphasized? Using the following scale, put a number next to each
set of characteristics:

---

1. Occasionally   3. Frequently   5. Continuously
2. Fairly regularly 4. Very frequently

____ 1. Direction, purpose, role clarity
____ 2. Belonging, teamwork, affiliation
____ 3. Compensation, recognition, rewards
____ 4. Productivity, impact, achievement
____ 5. Standardization, measurement, objectivity
____ 6. Sensitivity, consideration, support
____ 7. Challenge, variety, stimulation
____ 8. Coordination, predictability, control

You should now transfer your scores on this list to the corresponding points in Figure 3. After marking each score, you can
connect the scores to create a profile.

Figure 2. Juxtaposed Proverbs Representing Values, Beliefs, and Strategies.

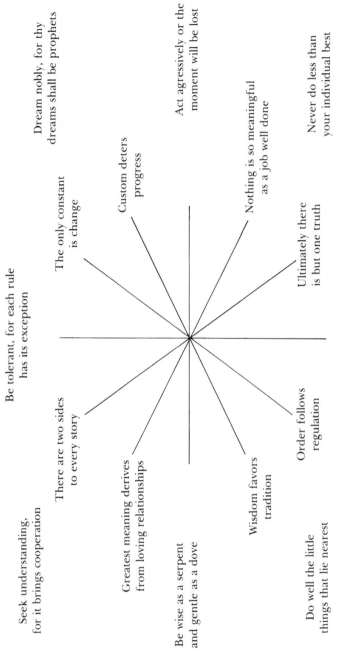

Figure 3. Juxtaposed Motives.

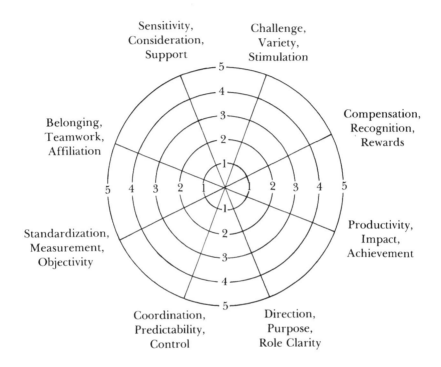

Attachment

Development

Security

Competence

Problem Solving. Finally, let us turn to your preferred methods for working on problems. Listed below are eight ways that a supervisor or manager might approach problems. Use the following scale to indicate how often you employ each one:

1. Seldom	3. Frequently	5. Almost always
2. Occasionally	4. Very frequently	

_____ 1. I recognize that there are often formal structures and processes. I like to solve problems by following stated rules and procedures.

_____ 2. I recognize that the world is often evolving. I like to identify new trends, possibilities, and opportunities, and I like to trust hunches, intuition, and insights.

_____ 3. I recognize that action and effort often result in achievement. I like to maintain a narrow focus so as not to be distracted from pursuing the highest priority.

_____ 4. I recognize that different perceptions are often held by different people. I like to show tolerance of diverse views and seek to synthesize them.

_____ 5. I recognize that there is often a best answer. I like to use accepted methods and rules to analyze tangible evidence and facts.

_____ 6. I recognize that organizational politics often surround decision processes. I like to negotiate with and influence significant power figures.

_____ 7. I recognize that there is often a need for clear direction. I like to establish rules, guidelines, and objectives.

_____ 8. I recognize that no two situations are alike. I like to show tolerance for and understanding of each unique case.

Again, your scores on the above eight questions should be transferred to the appropriate points in Figure 4. Do this by simply writing in the scores. As in Figure 3, you should connect the scores to create a profile.

Four Types of Information Processing

The three exercises are not independent. The four quadrants in each of the three figures reflect strong similarities as one moves from exercise to exercise. The quadrants suggest four different approaches to information processing. Drawing on the work of a variety of researchers (Forgus and Shulman, 1979; Driver and Rowe, 1979; Mitroff and Mason, 1982; Quinn and Rohrbaugh, 1983), we can describe each style or model.

Figure 4. Juxtaposed Problem Orientations.

I recognize that the world is evolving. I like to identify new trends, possibilities, and opportunities, and I like to trust hunches, intuition, and insight.

I recognize that organizational politics often surround decision processes. I like to negotiate with and influence significant power figures.

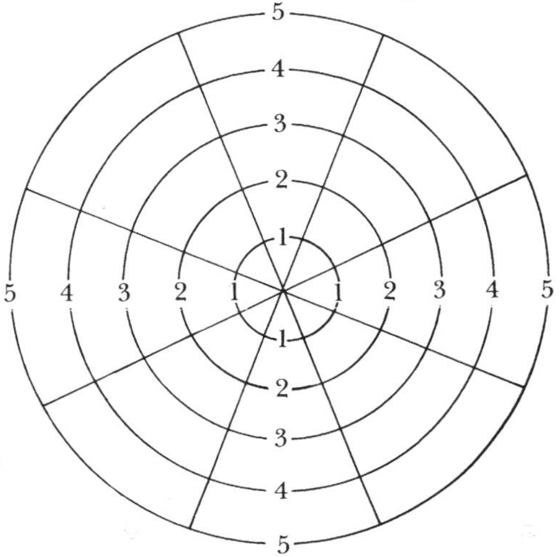

I recognize that action and effort often result in achievement. I like to maintain a narrow focus so as to not be distracted from pursuing the highest priority.

I recognize that no two situations are alike. I like to show tolerance for and understanding of each unique case.

I recognize that there is often a need for clear direction. I like to establish rules, guidelines, and objectives.

I recognize that different perceptions are often held by different people. I like to show tolerance of diverse views and seek to synthesize them.

I recognize that there are often formal structures and processes. I like to solve problems by following stated rules and procedures.

I recognize that there is often a best answer. I like to use accepted methods and rules to analyze tangible evidence and facts.

Rational Goal Approach. This model reflects the lower-right quadrant in the three exercises. Here we find a preference for short time lines and high certainty, as well as a need for independence and achievement. People in this mode tend to have a purposive orientation. They rely on a priori logic (known means-ends chains) and focus on the clarification of goals and structures. This is a very functional or instrumental outlook that tends toward the use of generalizations. People with this outlook tend to have a single purpose or focus when making decisions. They make rapid decisions and once the decision is made, it is final. This perspective is very achievement oriented and tends to emphasize logical direction and the initiation of action.

Developmental or Open Systems Approach. This approach reflects the upper-right quadrant in the three exercises. Here the preference is for short time lines and low certainty, and the need is for variation, risk, excitement, and growth. People in this mode tend to have an idealistic orientation. They rely on internally generated ideas, intuitions, and hunches. This tends to be a future-oriented approach that considers what might be. In processing information, individuals in this category tend to analyze the problems, cues, or messages from a dynamic, longitudinal view, and the subject is seen as if in a moving picture. In making decisions, people with this orientation tend to have a multiple focus. They make decisions very quickly but continue to gather information and adjust their decisions as they go along. The situation is an "open system," one that is influencing and being influenced by the environment. This subjective perspective is oriented toward creativity, risk, and growth. It tends to emphasize adaptability and external legitimacy.

But a cautionary note is necessary here. This approach to information processing is the one most consistent with flexible integration, action inquiry, or fluid processing of cues. It is not, however, the key to mastery. People who have this approach as a natural style may be quite blind to other approaches. They may have great difficulty, for example, functioning in highly routinized situations. This may be why some of the highly complex managers identified by Streufert and Swezey (1986), those with the high cognitive complexity discussed in Chapter One of this volume, cannot function well in highly stable situations. While a master manager may often use this approach, he or she will be able to drop it when appropriate and take up another approach. The master manager transcended style so as to not be blinded by it.

Consensual or Team Approach. This approach reflects the upper-left quadrant in the three exercises. Here the preference is for long time lines and low certainty, and the need is for affiliation and mutual dependence. This mode is oriented to feelings. It is a process-oriented view that suggests that the world can only be known through human interaction. Meaning is discovered through process. The individual case is more important than the general rule; hence, there is a high tolerance for individual exceptions and spontaneous events and behaviors. In making decisions, people with this outlook tend to have a multiple focus. They take the time to seek out diverse opinions and search for solutions that integrate the various positions. This perspective is oriented to affiliation and tends to emphasize harmony and consideration of individuals.

Hierarchical or Internal Process Approach. This approach reflects the lower-left quadrant in the three exercises. Here the preference is for long time lines and high certainty, and the need is for predictability and security. This objective perspective is oriented toward empiricism or the systematic examination of externally generated facts. It tends to be a present-oriented approach that describes what is. In processing information, people in this mode tend to analyze the focal problem, cue, or message from a static, cross-sectional view, and the subject is seen as if in a photograph, that is, as if it were frozen in time. In making decisions, people with this orientation tend to have a single focus. They take a long time to gather and systematically or scientifically analyze the facts. The objective is to obtain the single best answer or optimal solution. This hierarchical perspective is oriented toward security, order, and routinization and tends to emphasize standardization and perpetuation of the status quo. In organizations there is a focus on internal processes.

Normally, these four approaches are thought of as mutually exclusive. They are often measured by instruments such as that employed in exercise one. A person taking these tests is forced to make choices between items and will find himself falling completely in one area or another (usually in one of the quadrants).

But this approach to measurement is quite limited. People operate in all four quadrants, even the quadrant that they like least. I therefore prefer to use measurements such as those in exercises two and three. These produce a profile covering all the quadrants. In taking this both/and rather than either/or approach, we usually find that what is important is not people's "strong quadrant" but their "weak quadrant." It is in this quadrant that people tend to distort reality. The values from the weak quadrant are the ones that are most likely to be jettisoned. It is these items that get ignored or negatively redefined.

How We Think About Organizing and Managing

Information-processing styles can be helpful in understanding why people have difficulty in seeing the contradictory expectations that occur in organizations. Over the history of organizational theory, four notions of organizing have emerged that closely parallel the four information-processing orientations. These are the general frames or perspectives that people have, that is, the assumptions they make when they think about "good" management. As we shall eventually see, they are far more than simple abstractions about organizing; in fact, we can call them powerful moral positions that influence every aspect of organizational life.

The Hierarchy. Perhaps the oldest and most pervasive notion of organization is that of a hierarchy. In organizational studies the description of this form begins with Max Weber's (1921) writings on bureaucracy. The strength of this model of organizing is that a hierarchy provides stability and predictability. In a hierarchy there is great emphasis on measurement, documentation, and information management. People are given well-defined roles and are expected to follow rules that outline what they should do. The major reward for their efforts is job security. Hierarchies seem to function best when the task to be done is well understood and when time is not an important factor. The expectations around the hierarchy are the preferences reflected in the internal process model. From this perspective, managers are expected to play two primary roles. They are expected to monitor and to coordinate.

As a monitor, a manager is expected to know what is going on in the unit, to determine if people are complying with the rules, and to see if the unit is meeting its quotas. The monitor knows all the facts and details and is good at quantitative analysis. Behaviors in this role include handling paper work, reviewing and responding to routine information, and carrying out inspections, tours, and reviews of printouts and reports.

As a coordinator, a manager is expected to maintain the structure and flow of the system. The person in this role is expected to be dependable and reliable. Behaviors include various forms of work facilitation such as scheduling, organizing, and coordinating staff efforts, handling crises, and attending to technological, logistical, and housekeeping issues.

The Firm. Perhaps the next most common notion of organizing is that of the firm. Here the system is seen as a rational economic tool. The major emphasis is on profit or the bottom line. There is an underlying theory of rational action. It assumes that goal clarification results in productive action. Tasks are clarified, objectives are set, and action is taken. Here people are clearly instructed by a decisive authority figure and are rewarded financially if they perform well. If they do not, they are asked to leave. This system seems to assume task clarity and short time horizons. The expectations around the firm are the preferences reflected in the rational goal model. In this model, managers are expected to direct and to produce.

As a director, a manager is expected to clarify expectations through processes such as planning and goal setting and to be a decisive initiator who defines problems, selects alternatives, establishes objectives, defines roles and tasks, generates rules and policies, evaluates performance, and gives instructions.

A producer is expected to be task oriented and work focused and to have high interest, motivation, energy, and personal drive. Here a manager is supposed to accept responsibility, complete assignments, and maintain high personal productivity. This usually involves motivating members to increase production and to accomplish stated goals.

The Adhocracy. Another concept of organizing has emerged in the last fifteen years. During this period terms such as *organic system, flat system, loosely coupled system, matrix,* and *temporary system* have been used to describe this way of organizing. The central strength of this model is that it fosters adaptability and change. There is great emphasis on innovation and creativity, that is, on doing things that have never been done before. Here people are not controlled but are inspired. They are part of a collectivity attempting to do something of great importance. Motivation is seldom an issue. People feel fully committed and fully challenged. If they succeed in implementing a new vision, considerable external recognition and resources will follow. Adhocracies function best when the task is not well understood and when there is great urgency about completing it. The expectations around the adhocracy are the preferences contained in the open systems model. Here managers are expected to be innovators and brokers.

As an innovator, a manager is expected to facilitate adaptation and change. The innovator absorbs uncertainty by monitoring the outside environment, identifying important trends, and conceptualizing and projecting needed changes. Unlike the monitor role where deduction, facts, and quantitative analysis rule, the innovator role requires the manager to rely on induction, ideas, and intuitive insights. In this role the manager is expected to be a creative, clever dreamer who sees the future, envisions innovations, packages them in inviting ways, and convinces others that they are necessary and desirable.

In a system that deals with the external environment, politics becomes important, and the manager must begin to play the broker role. The broker is particularly concerned with maintaining external legitimacy and obtaining external resources. Here the manager is expected to be politically astute, persuasive, influential, and powerful. Image, appearance, and reputation are important. The manager is expected to meet with people from outside the unit, to represent the company and market its product or services, to act as a liaison and spokesperson, and to acquire resources.

The Team. Since the beginning of the human relations movement, people have talked about the importance of consensus, cohesion, and teamwork. In the last few years, interest has centered on Japanese methods for achieving teamwork. Much has been written, for example, about the virtues of clans (Ouchi, 1981). With the team approach to organizing, the emphasis is on human resources and the development of commitment. Here there is a great emphasis on information sharing and participative decision making. People are seen not as isolated individuals but as cooperating members of a common social system with a common stake in what happens. They are held together by a sense of affiliation and belonging. Here managers are expected to be facilitators and mentors.

The facilitator is expected to foster collective effort, to build cohesion and teamwork, and to manage interpersonal conflict. In this role the leader is described as process oriented. Expected behaviors include intervening in interpersonal disputes, using conflict reduction techniques, developing cohesion and morale, obtaining input and participation, and facilitating group problem solving.

But the manager is also expected to be a mentor, to engage in the development of people through a caring, empathetic orientation. In this role the leader must be helpful, considerate, sensitive, approachable, open, and fair. He or she listens, supports legitimate requests, conveys appreciation, and gives compliments and credit. People are resources to be developed. The leader helps with skill building, provides training opportunities, and helps people develop plans for their own individual development.

Contradictions

At first, these four models for organizing may appear to be four very unrelated and very academic statements. They are neither. First, they are deeply related and interwoven. Pick any one and it will turn out to be opposite to one of the others and a complement to the two that remain. The expectations in the rational goal model (the firm), for example, are in stark contrast to the expectations in the human relations model (the team). Further, they complement the expectations in the internal process model (the hierarchy) and the open systems model (the adhocracy). Likewise, the expectations in the open systems model are in stark contrast to the expectations in the internal process model but are complementary with the two remaining models. This characteristic of competing assumptions and expectations is one to which we will return often.

Second, the four models are not simply another set of academic abstractions but representations of four competing moralities, four ways of seeing the world that people hold implicitly and about which they feel intensely. They represent the values that precede the assumptions that people make about what is good and what is bad, the unseen values for whose sake people, programs, policies, and organizations live and die.

Real organizations do not fall neatly into one or the other of these four models. In fact, the models do not contain organizations, organizations contain the models, all of them. In every organization all four models exist. Managers are expected to play all of these roles and to simultaneously consider and balance the competing demands that are represented by each set of expectations. Theories of management, because they must be internally consistent, tend not to tolerate such a paradoxical notion. Likewise, the advice given by practicing managers, because it also must be internally consistent, tends not to contain such contradiction.

Finally, the four modes of thinking and organizing are

tied to the four phases in the transformational cycle in Chapter Two. People who are weak in the rational-goal approach may have difficulty in the initiation phase. Those who are weak in the developmental approach may have difficulty in the uncertainty phase. Likewise, weakness in the consensual approach may lead to difficulties in the transformational phase, and weakness in the hierarchical approach may lead to difficulties in the routinization phase.

Because of their information-processing styles, both managers and theorists shave away the values in their weak quadrants. The masters of management, by contrast, manage to become purposive without becoming schismogenic. They pursue one set of values while looking for cues that will signal the need to shift to another, sometimes directly contradictory, set of values. They are able to see and work with the contradictions in organizations. This, the seeing of contradictions in the organizing process, is the topic to which we turn in the next chapter.

4

The Competing Values Model:
Redefining Organizational
Effectiveness and Change

A few years ago I was invited to visit with the chief executive officer of a fast-growing high-tech firm. He recounted the following story:

> It started out like any other meeting. I made the point that conflicts seemed to be occurring more frequently than ever before and suggested that we make a list of our problems. After two or three minutes of listing problems, the tension mounted considerably. Nearly every item on the list suggested the need for some kind of reorganization. A few people wanted to maintain the status quo while others wanted change. Some argued for centralization. Some argued for decentralization. Various individuals began to take stronger and stronger opposing views. Finally our finance person accused our information systems director of trying to take over the organization. It caused an explosion. Everyone was screaming at once. It was chaos. Everyone had a diagnosis of what was wrong and everyone had a solution, but nobody's diagnosis or solution agreed with anyone else's. After that session I decided that we needed some outside help.

How to organize? In the abstract, the question seems very straightforward. In reality, it is often a difficult one to answer or even to discuss. Why should this be true? First of all, resources are usually at stake. Second, and perhaps more important, we are unaware of the strong predispositions we have. Each of us tends to have unconscious values, as discussed in the preceding chapter, that tell us the "right" way to organize and manage. These values can lead to much confusion.

In the preceding chapter I argued that organizations are complex and dynamic, that they are settings in which managers must fulfill many competing expectations. I argued that in every organization there are at least four general perspectives on what "good" organizations are and what "good" managers do. Unfortunately, at the perceptual level, these perspectives are contradictory. They are also emotionally held "moral" positions. People feel strongly about them, and it is often difficult for them to see any value in contrasting views. Because values tend to be implicit, most people are unaware that they are carrying around an ideal set of preferences about organizing and that there may also be advantages to be gained in directly opposite preferences. These preferences usually go unarticulated. Instead, they tend to be expressed as blind moral statements that reflect anger over conflicts within the organization: "John is too softhearted, he is running this place like a country club"; "Sue is a pigheaded dictator, she runs this place like a prison camp."

I also said that as managers become masters, they develop the ability to see more cues or stimuli than those who are less sophisticated. They see these cues as moving flows. They learn to focus on the most important cues and then develop a conscious plan based on a particular set of values. They keep to this plan while observing other cues, and, when appropriate, they drop the old plan in favor of another plan. This new plan may reflect a contradictory set of values. That is, these managers have the capacity to see problems from contradictory frames, to entertain and pursue alternative perspectives. Over time, in the process of becoming a master manager, a person begins to understand that there are contrasting frames of organizing and that there are advantages and disadvantages to each. The manager begins to transcend her personal style in the sense that she comes to appreciate and use approaches that initially were not natural to her. The manager discovers the contradictory nature of organizing.

For most of us, discovering the contradictory nature of organizing is not easy. We have biases in how we process information, and we prefer to live in certain kinds of settings. Our biases are further influenced by our organizational experience at both the functional and cultural levels. At the functional level, for example, accountants and marketing people tend to develop very different assumptions about what is "good." At the cultural level, there is often a set of values that conveys "how we do things around here." Because these values tend to be so powerful, it is very difficult to see past them without being schismogenic; that is, it is difficult to recognize that there are weaknesses in our own perspective and advantages in opposing perspectives. It is particularly difficult to realize that these various perspectives must be understood, juxtaposed, and blended in a delicate, complex, and dynamic way. It is much more natural to see them as either/or positions in which one must triumph over the other.

In this chapter we will attempt to more fully comprehend the notion of organizations as contradictory systems. I will begin by reviewing a framework of competing values. I will first show how it can be used to diagnose an organization from both static and dynamic perspectives. Finally, in Chapter Nine, you will learn how to diagnose your own organization.

Competing Values Model

In the last chapter I described four perspectives on organizing. Here I will not treat them as four separate orientations but try to see them within an integrated framework in which their relationships will become clear. In order to do so I will briefly review their historical development.

In the late seventies and early eighties, many of my colleagues and I became interested in the issue of organizational effectiveness. We were asking the question, What are the characteristics of effective organizations? Many studies were done in which people set out to measure the characteristics of organizations. These measures were then submitted to a technique called *factor analysis*. It produced lists of variables that characterized effective organizations. The problem was that these variables differed from one study to another. It seemed that the more we learned, the less we knew.

My colleague, John Rohrbaugh, and I therefore tried to reframe the question. Instead of asking what effective organizations looked like, we decided to ask how experts think about effective organizations. This would allow us to get to the assumptions behind the studies and perhaps make sense of what was causing the confusion. In a series of studies (Quinn and Rohrbaugh, 1983), we had organizational theorists and researchers make judgments regarding the similarity or dissimilarity between pairs of effectiveness criteria. The data were analyzed using a technique called *multidimensional scaling*. Results of the analyses suggested that organizational theorists and researchers share an implicit theoretical framework, or cognitive map (Figure 5).

Note that the two axes in the figure create four quadrants. The vertical axis ranges from flexibility to control, the horizontal axis from an internal to an external focus. Each quadrant of the framework represents one of the four major models in organization theory. The human relations model, for example, stresses criteria such as those in the upper-left quadrant: cohesion and morale, along with human resource development. The open systems model stresses criteria such as those in the upper-right quadrant. These include flexibility and readiness as well as growth, resource acquisition, and external support. The rational goal model stresses the kind of criteria found in the lower-right quadrant, including planning and goal setting and productivity and efficiency. The internal process model is represented in the lower-left quadrant. It stresses information management and communication, along with stability and control.

Each model has a polar opposite. The human relations model, which emphasizes flexibility and internal focus, stands in stark contrast to the rational goal model, which stresses

Figure 5. Competing Values Framework: Effectiveness.

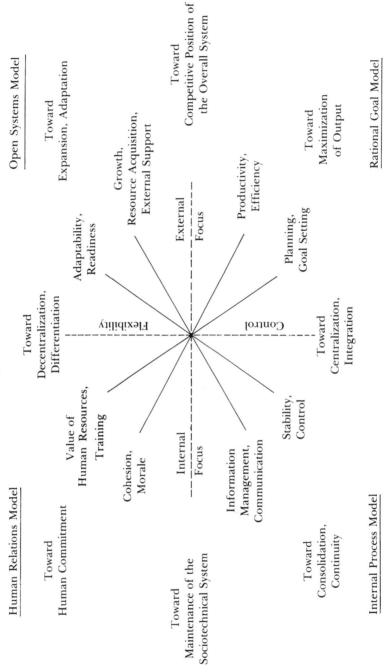

control and external focus. The open systems model, which is characterized by flexibility and external focus, runs counter to the internal process model, which emphasizes control and internal focus. Parallels among the models are also important. The human relations and open systems models share an emphasis on flexibility. The open systems and rational goal models have an external focus (responding to outside change and producing in a competitive market). The rational goal and internal process models are rooted in the value of control. Finally, the internal process and human relations models share an internal focus (concern for the human and technical systems inside the organization).

Each of the models reflects an orientation to an information-processing style and a resulting bias toward one of the modes of organizing discussed in Chapter Three. The two sets of criteria in each quadrant also suggest the implicit means-ends theory that is associated with each mode. Thus, the rational goal model is associated with the mode of organizing that I labeled the *firm mode*. Here planning and goal setting are viewed as a means of achieving productivity and efficiency. In the open systems model we find the adhocracy, where adaptability and readiness are viewed as a means to growth, resource acquisition, and external support. In the internal process model is the hierarchy, where information management and communication are viewed as a means of arriving at stability and control. In the human relations quadrant we find the team. Here cohesion and morale are viewed as a means of increasing the value of human resources.

This scheme is called the *competing values framework* because the criteria seem to initially carry a conflictual message. We want our organizations to be adaptable and flexible, but we also want them to be stable and controlled. We want growth, resource acquisition, and external support, but we also want tight information management and formal communication. We want an emphasis on the value of human resources, but we also want an emphasis on planning and goal setting. The model does not suggest that these oppositions cannot mutually exist in a real system. It suggests, rather, that these criteria, values, and assumptions are oppositions in our minds. We tend to think that they are very different from one another, and we sometimes assume them to be mutually exclusive.

Over time, we have applied the model to many different problems. As these applications were made, we learned that the model would have more utility if we made some minor adaptations. In considering organizational culture, for instance, the model is adapted as shown in Figure 6. Here the indicators of performance are slightly elaborated and modified. Of particular significance are the labels on the horizontal axis. It gradually became clearer to us that the external focus reflected an orientation toward competition, engagement, urgency, or short time lines. The internal focus reflected an orientation toward maintenance, coordination, equilibrium, or longer time lines. In Figure 6 the models and organizational types are labeled in each quadrant.

The Framework as a Diagnostic Tool: A Static Perspective

The competing values framework can be used to diagnose and intervene in actual organizations. As an example, let us once again focus on the high-tech firm whose managers were unable to agree on how to reorganize. After interviewing a sample of organization members, our consulting team suggested that an executive retreat might be useful, and this suggestion was accepted. At the retreat the organization's management team, working with us as external consultants, initiated a planning process designed to deal with the increasingly frequent problems centering on the organization's planning, staff development, and information management capabilities. We assisted the executive group in making a seven-hour diagnosis of the performance characteristics of the organization. The first task in this diagnosis was administration of a questionnaire measuring the concepts in the competing values framework (see instrumentation in Chapter Nine). Scores from the management team were averaged to create the group profile of the organization's orientation as shown in Figure 7.

The second task in the analysis involved using this organi-

Figure 6. Competing Values Framework: Culture.

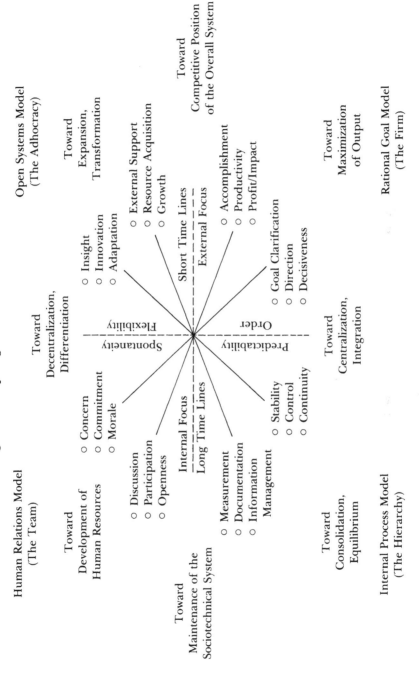

Figure 7. Profile of a High-Tech Firm.

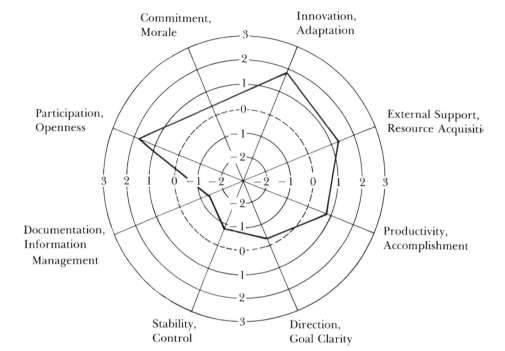

zational profile to generate a list of possible steps for future action. After discussing the profile, the group worked to generate lists of action statements for each quadrant of the competing values model.

The generation and discussion of the action statements did much to clarify the meaning of the profile and to aid in assessing the capacity of the organization. There follows a summary of this discussion, organized around the four quadrants of the competing values model. Before reading that summary, however, you may want to make your own interpretation of the profile. (The standard scores are based on a diverse national sample of organizational units.)

Open Systems Model. We concluded that the organization was very good at adjusting to changes and to sudden crises, but we felt some concern over its ability to move into new areas of activity in a timely, systematic fashion. Several statements suggested the need for a decision system and an organization structure that would support and preserve flexibility and stimulate innovation. The need to be careful about "buying flexibility at the cost of internal integrity" was also emphasized. In considering growth, the executive team expressed great concern about getting the expansion process under control. There were a number of statements about planned growth — for example, about the need to link growth patterns to the goals of the organization, to develop a capacity for program development, research, and analysis, and, in general, to take a more comprehensive, thoughtful, and "whole organization" approach to expansion.

Rational Goal Model. In considering productivity, the members of the group first pointed out the need for stronger second-level management. For a number of reasons, they felt that it was very difficult to delegate key tasks to subordinates, with the result that the executive team found itself overburdened. They also indicated a need for the development of standards in the areas of quality control and production, as well as a need for the clarification of goals. The group pointed out the need to set aside a regular time for formalized, timely planning with wide involvement and a commitment to stick with specified objectives. They also came to realize that the company had to establish clearer time lines and benchmarks for major activities and for a more effective link between the budget-making and planning processes.

Internal Process Model. Of all the quadrants, the one in the lower left appeared to be most neglected by the organization. In the discussion of stability control, it became clear that internal coordination was an area of growing concern to company executives. They called for clearer specification of role expectations and job descriptions and for procedures to resolve conflict over internal resources such as copying and word processing. The need for consolidation and standardization in certain units was also addressed. In the area of documentation and information management, it was agreed that a number of changes were needed. These included the formal recording of certain policies and procedures, the establishment of a corporate file system, the development of data banks, and a cutback on unnecessary paper flow. It was also agreed that there was a need for increased sharing of verbal information, and a number of mechanisms for achieving this were suggested.

Human Relations Model. For some time the organization had prided itself on its high cohesion and morale. It was, therefore, very unsettling when some members made convincing arguments that morale was falling off, particularly at levels below the executive team. Suggestions for addressing the problem were to hold more staff meetings, to hold unit retreats, and to shift evaluation and budgeting functions to the unit heads. It was also argued that morale would improve if the organization took the following steps: increase hiring, provide more effective training and development, establish a better salary and reward system, develop career ladders, do better matching of skills and jobs, and increase delegation.

Once the profile and supporting information had been generated, the members of the group agreed that they had made a comprehensive diagnosis of the organization. They thought it would then be possible to prioritize problems and to begin exploring solutions. (In Chapter Nine and the appendixes are the materials necessary to provide a profile of your own organization.)

The Framework from a Dynamic Perspective

Throughout this book I have argued that master managers have the capacity to see complex and dynamic patterns. The diagnosis given above was done from a static, cross-sectional, or one-time perspective; in other words, the organization was viewed as though it were a photograph. Such a perspective, however, can fail to uncover some very important facts. In the case of the organization discussed above, something crucial was happening that no one in the organization understood, and the analysis did not reveal what it was. I will return to this organization and its hidden problem, but when I do so, it will be from a dynamic perspective.

I might begin our examination of this perspective by noting that the values emphasized in an organization change over time. Often these changes come as crises. In the early stages of development, some of them can be predicted, as the story of still another organization illustrates.

Several years ago we did a study of a developmental center in the mental health system of the state of New York. Serving a six-county area, the organization provided care for children with developmental disorders and for the retarded of all ages. From its beginning, the center was directed by a psychiatrist who was nationally known for his writings and work in the area of community mental health. He was a charismatic leader who tended to generate either extreme loyalty or extreme opposition. Both supporters and critics, however, agreed that he had a genius for conceptualizing innovative solutions to the problems of service delivery.

The director's past work and writings in community mental health had generated a series of prescriptions for the treatment of the mentally disabled. These prescriptions became the organization's ideology. Collectively, they were called the *developmental treatment model*. This model emphasized the broad participation of parents, consumers, and the community and focused on the development of independence and self-reliance in clients. This developmental ideology was the cutting edge of the "deinstitutionalization" movement that was then sweeping the mental health profession.

The center was composed of seven teams and a support group. Although the teams were relatively autonomous, they followed a common set of guidelines. The teams included numerous disciplines (social work, child psychiatry, special education, pediatrics, psychology, rehabilitation counseling, and so on) and were staffed so as to maintain a balance among at least four areas: social-recreational, psychological, educational-vocational, and health care. For every professional hired, at least one person from the community (with a bachelor's degree or less) also had to be hired. After conducting the first series of interviews in our study, we entered the following description in our field report:

> The team is a fluid, nonbureaucratic system with the capacity to immediately assign and reassign staff in response to changing organizational needs. Even the use of the administrators is characterized by flexibility since they often have more than one organizational role. The organization appears to have been very successful in identifying needs and reorganizing staff and other resources to meet these needs. The organization has been well matched to the characteristics of the environment and the nature of the task. In general, the staff expressed satisfaction with the fluid and informal nature of the organization and the subsequent freedom, responsibility, and room for creativity that this type of organization facilitates. This is reflected in the fact that they habitually spend long hours at work, work weekends, carry out multiple organizational roles, and expand or stretch their talents and influences almost beyond a point of reason. This almost missionary dedication and zeal is infectious and is a valuable tactical tool in their dealings with the community.

In short, the organizational structure was a reflection of the philosophy of its director. For example, the director had no office, but would go wherever he thought he was needed and establish a temporary base of operations there. Strong emphasis was placed on openness, cooperation, creativity, and innovation. While the director reserved a veto power over group decisions, he seldom used it, and most major decisions were arrived at through participative decision-making techniques. The physical plants of some teams were intentionally kept small, in the belief that overcrowding would encourage members to be out in the community rather than in their offices. Dress standards and strict attention to seniority were not considered important. The chain of command was not easily identifiable, and there was a heavy emphasis on face-to-face communication rather than on formal written documents. The organic or ambiguous nature of the structure was reflected by the fact that, despite attempts to do so, no one had been able to draw up an organizational chart that satisfactorily reflected the functioning of the organization.

Within the organization, there was a high concern for the accomplishment of purposes as set forth in the developmental model. This required an emphasis on establishing inter-organizational relationships and capturing external support. As our initial field report put it: "The team has been very successful in marshaling the energies of its own workers and those of the community to develop and provide an array of services to the retarded not available theretofore. Both the staff and the community workers exhibited a high degree of cohesion and an intense dedication to the Cause. It was our observation that a good deal of the community's interest was a result of the zeal of the staff of the team. The team has been very successful in identifying and obtaining monies from various sources, including appropriations from the Department of Mental Hygiene, the legislature, grant monies from the federal government, as well as convincing community agencies to redeploy some of their monies to service for the retarded."

Soon after the above entry was written, however, one of the two major newspapers serving the area, the *Albany Times Union*, began to run an extensive exposé of the entire New York State Department of Mental Hygiene (DMH) of which this organization was a part. Entitled "Wasted Dollars/Wasted Lives" (1979), the series included numerous devastating reports about bureaucratic inefficiency at the central office of the DMH and numerous descriptions of the bleak aspects of life in its institutions. Initially, the developmental center was mentioned only in summary statements. But it eventually became one of the primary points of focus in the series. Day after day blistering attacks on the management of the center appeared in the paper.

Nearly all these attacks focused on violations of state rules and procedures.

The program had been under heavy pressure for four months when it was finally announced that the director had been asked by the commissioner of mental hygiene to take a six-week leave while a departmental probe was conducted. The investigation was to center on administrative and personnel practices at the center. Six weeks later the results of the probe were made public. Findings criticized the director for failing to provide direction, to set up a traditional organization structure, and to implement other necessary controls. It also recommended that the top-level administrative staff be relieved of their duties.

The report was met with outrage by supporters of the director. They accused the DMH of carrying out a vendetta. Moreover, a newspaper article reported that the governor, lieutenant governor, and several state legislators had expressed concern to the commissioner that the director get a "fair shake." When the probe was finally completed, the director was reinstated and given one year to address a list of problems. Most of these had to do with establishing clear lines of authority and clearly identifiable roles for staff members, with following rules and regulations, and with setting up mechanisms to ensure accountability and control.

Shortly after the year was over, the founding director left the state, and he was replaced with a "more administratively minded" director. Thereafter many staff members also left. By the end of the next year, there were few people working in jobs for which they were overqualified, the missionary zeal had disappeared, and the center began to function in a more controlled manner. As the system became increasingly formalized, staff members reported a falloff in commitment, productivity, and flexibility.

A Model of Transition in Young Organizations

What was happening? In attempting to understand the above process, a colleague and I used the competing values framework to develop a model for describing transitions in young organizations (Quinn and Cameron, 1983).

As indicated in Figure 8, there seem to be four distinct transitional stages in the development of new organizations, namely, the entrepreneurial, collectivity, formalization, and elaboration stages. In the entrepreneurial stage—typified by innovation, creativity, and the marshaling of resources—the strongest emphasis appears to be on open systems criteria of effectiveness. That is, the success of an organization will tend to be associated with its flexibility, growth, resource acquisition, and development of external support. The achievement of a "survival threshold" and the stabilization of resources are prerequisites for organizational success. "Dreaming" and entrepreneurship are activities necessary to get the organization off the ground.

As shown in Figure 8, open systems criteria are also important in other life cycle stages, but they appear to be particularly important during the initial stage. Organizational success tends to be defined in the entrepreneurial stage primarily by how well the organization meets criteria of growth, resource acquisition, external support, and adaptability.

Organizations in the collectivity stage appear to be characterized by the criteria associated with the human relations model. This stage is typified by informal communication and structure, a sense of family and cooperation among members, a high degree of commitment by members, and personalized leadership. We are not suggesting that human relations criteria are the only relevant criteria during the collectivity stage of development or that human relations criteria are not important in other developmental stages as well. Rather, we are pointing out that human relations criteria appear to dominate in defining organizational effectiveness in this stage and that they are more important in the collectivity stage than in any other stage.

In the formalization stage, organizational stability, efficiency of production, rules and procedures, and conservative trends typify organizations. Effectiveness appears to be defined primarily on the basis of criteria in the internal process and rational goal models, that is, by goal setting

Figure 8. Life Cycles of Successful Young Organizations.

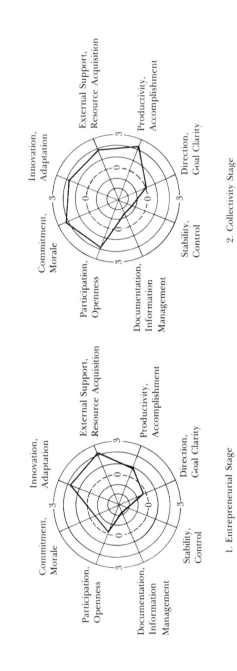

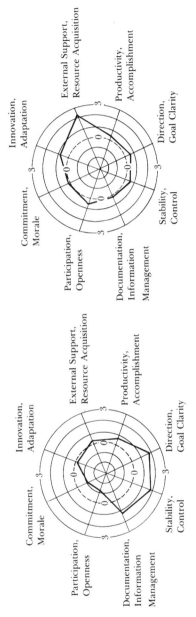

External Support,
Resource Acquisition

Innovation,
Adaptation

Productivity,
Accomplishment

Commitment,
Morale

Direction,
Goal Clarity

Participation,
Openness

Stability,
Control

Documentation,
Information
Management

4. Elaboration of Structure Stage

Open Systems Model

External Support,
Resource Acquisition

Innovation,
Adaptation

Productivity,
Accomplishment

Commitment,
Morale

Direction,
Goal Clarity

Participation,
Openness

Stability,
Control

Documentation,
Information
Management

3. Formalization Stage

Human Relations Model

and goal attainment, productivity, efficiency, information management-communication, and stability-control. While goal accomplishment, productivity, and efficiency are clearly important through most of the life cycle of an organization, it is in the formalization stage that these rational model criteria are most emphasized.

In the fourth stage—elaboration of structure—the organization monitors the external environment in order to renew itself or expand its domain, or both. Decentralization of structure occurs, and a balance between differentiation and integration is necessary at this stage. While there appears to be at least moderate emphasis on internal process criteria, human relations criteria, and rational goal model criteria, the heaviest emphasis is put on the open systems model, which emphasizes flexibility, resource acquisition, and growth.

Explaining What Happened

As seen in Figure 8, in the entrepreneurial and collectivity stages, the most important criteria of effectiveness are those of the open systems model and the human relations model. During these stages there is less emphasis on rational goal criteria and on internal process criteria. With the onset of the formalization stage, however, there is a dramatic shift in criteria. Information management, stability, control, productivity, and goal setting become increasingly important. Not surprisingly, this shift is accompanied by a dramatic decline in the emphasis on open systems and human relations criteria.

In the history of the developmental center just provided, there is evidence to suggest that the changes in the dominant criteria of organizational effectiveness followed the predicted pattern. The center started out in the entrepreneurial stage and continued into the collectivity stage with the management team, led by the director, in undisputed control. The criteria of success that were most valued by this group were consistent with the implementation of an innovative treatment model. As such, formalization and control were not only unimportant criteria, they were contradictory to the organization's accepted values.

The major criteria of effectiveness (creativity, informality, and morale) for this group, therefore, became accepted as part of the organization's self-definition.

For a time, the group was successful in warding off controls and the power plays of others. However, the attack by the *Times Union* allowed other political interests to coalesce and become dominant. That is, a new constituency acquired power over the previously dominant management group. This created an overwhelming pressure toward formalization in the organization because the criteria of effectiveness valued by the new constituency included efficiency, control, planning, and so on (these are criteria consistent with the formalization stage). The organization found it necessary to adopt these new criteria of success in order to survive, and this in turn necessitated a change in its structure and activities. However wrenching it may be, this phenomenon occurs regularly in both public- and private-sector organizations.

The move from the collectivity stage to the formalization stage is an extremely difficult one for new organizations to make. For most, this first major crisis takes on the air of a mysterious, even tragic drama. Unfortunately, the members of the organization are not dispassionate observers in the audience, but inexperienced, onstage actors, trying to perform without a script in a rapidly unfolding drama. Hence, the problem of transition can be costly in both financial and human terms. There is often a falloff in performance, as well as prolonged conflict among members of the organization. They fail to understand that a predictable macro process is occurring and instead see their painful experience as idiosyncratic. They interpret it through a micro lens and look for individuals and groups to blame. Each coalition chooses a different scapegoat: the external interests with their "evil intentions" to destroy a system they do not understand or appreciate, the top administrator's "inability to manage," the core group's "naivete" in attempting to maintain the original ideology, the bureaucratically oriented new members and their lack of "appreciation" for the "real purpose" of the organization. Each group becomes schismogenic.

Revisiting the High-Tech Firm

When I last mentioned the high-tech firm, I noted that there were some things that our analysis, made from a single point in time, did not reveal. It turns out that the organization was facing this same transition from the collectivity to the formalization stage. After assisting in the analysis at the management retreat, we wanted to help the executives learn how to take a dynamic perspective on themselves. To that end we developed diagrams and prepared a presentation.

The executives found our presentation very interesting. They agreed that they were going through the shift from stage 2 to stage 3. They were able to recognize and identify patterns that they had not before fully understood. They reexamined the needs that they had identified through the internal process model, and they were able to articulate strategies that would help them through the formalization crisis.

We were very excited and very proud of our work with the firm. Imagine our surprise when, a few months later, we learned that most of the members of the top management team had been asked to leave the company.

The formalization crisis had fully played itself out, and our help had made little difference. Why? Because we had impacted the group intellectually but not emotionally. They could understand, repeat, and even espouse the ideas we gave them, but they could not practice these ideas. Emotionally the ideas around formalization were repugnant to these people. The values in the lower-left corner of Figure 8 were "morally" wrong. They were a denial of everything that the group believed in and found worthwhile. Thus, these executives lost their jobs because they were schismogenic. They could not read the changing cues and reframe their beliefs about what the firm needed at this point in its development. They could not fully understand, accept, and act on the notion that success breeds failure and that their old strategies needed to be drastically modified.

The notion of being too successful is hard to understand, and the notion that success generates failure is even harder to understand. Yet this is exactly what often happens to managers and organizations. Situations change while managers keep pressing the same buttons that worked in the past. On the one hand, the creative manager tries to avoid formalization by becoming still more innovative. The increased innovation creates a still greater need for control. On the other hand, the highly structured manager meets the signals for change by increasing control, and this, in turn, results in still more pressure for change. The system eventually goes into crisis because too much emphasis has been placed on a given set of values. It has not developed the capacity to simultaneously pursue opposites, and this inability drives the organization into an ineffective negative zone and eventually into crisis. In the next chapter we will attempt to better understand this phenomenon.

5

The Failure of Success:
How Good Becomes Bad

In the last chapter I introduced the notion that people can get trapped by the logic of success and that the continual pursuit of a sound strategy sometimes results in failure. A manager who pursues the right strategy may nevertheless find that the situation continues to get worse. He or she has unknowingly created a vicious cycle that results in a paradoxical phenomenon. Positive values become negative. For example, innovation, adaptation, and change become premature responsiveness and disastrous experimentation. Stability, control, and continuity become habitual perpetuation and ironbound tradition. Good becomes bad. In this chapter I attempt to explain this process. The chapter begins by examining the culture of organizations and exploring the paradoxical transformation of values. Finally, I consider the difference between individuals who are destroyed by success and those who are not.

How Values Manifest Themselves

In recent years much has been written about culture in organizations. When we think of the manifestation of values in organizations, it is their cultures that we are thinking of. Simply put, culture is the set of values and assumptions that underlie the statement, "This is how we do things around here." Culture at the organizational level, like information processing at the individual level, tends to take on moral overtones. While cultures tend to vary dramatically, they share the common characteristic of providing integration of effort in one direction while often sealing off the possibility of moving in another direction. An illustration may be helpful.

In October 1980 *Business Week* ran an article contrasting the cultures at J. C. Penney and PepsiCo. At Penney's the culture focuses on the values of fairness and long-term loyalty. Indeed, a manager was once chewed out by the president of the company for making *too much money!* To do so was unfair to the customers, and at Penney's one must never take advantage of the customer. Customers are free to return merchandise with which they are not satisfied. Suppliers know that they can establish stable, long-term relationships with Penney's. Employees know that if their ability to perform a given job begins to deteriorate, they will not find themselves out on the street; rather, an appropriate alternative position will be found for them.

The core of the company's culture is captured in "The Penney Idea." Although it was adopted in 1913, it is a very modern-sounding statement, consisting of seven points: "To serve the public, as nearly as we can, to its complete satisfaction; to expect for the service we render a fair remuneration and not all the profit the traffic will bear; to do all in our power to pack the customer's dollar full of value, quality, and satisfaction; to continue to train ourselves and our associates so that the service we give will be more and more intelligently performed; to improve constantly the human factor in our business; to reward men and women in our organization through participation in what the business produces; to test our every policy, method, and act in this wise: 'Does it square with what is right and just?'"

The culture at PepsiCo is in stark contrast to that at Penney's. After years as a sleepy company that took the back seat to Coca-Cola, PepsiCo underwent a major change by adopting a much more competitive culture. This new culture was manifest both externally and internally. On the outside PepsiCo directly confronted Coca-Cola. In bold ads customers were asked to taste and compare the products of the two companies. Internally, managers knew that their jobs were on the line and that they had to produce results. There was continuous pressure to show improvement in market share, product volume, and profits. Jobs were won or lost over a "tenth of a point" difference in these areas.

Staffs were kept small. Managers were constantly moved from job to job and expected to work long hours. The pressure never let up. During a blizzard, for example, the chief executive officer found a snowmobile and drove it to work. (This story is told regularly at PepsiCo.) Competitive team and individual sports are emphasized, and people are expected to stay in shape. The overall climate is reflected in the often repeated phrase, "We are the marines not the army."

The differences between these two companies could hardly be greater. Reading this account, you have probably concluded that one culture is more attractive than the other, and you would expect others to agree with your choice. But it is very likely that if you visited PepsiCo and spoke of "The Penney Idea," you would be laughed at. If you tried to press it upon PepsiCo employees, they would probably become incensed. Likewise, if you visited Penney's and described or tried to press upon them the values of PepsiCo, they would have the same reaction. You would be violating sacred assumptions.

Interestingly, the major problem at PepsiCo was seen as the absence of loyalty. Coca-Cola's response to the PepsiCo attack, for example, was to hire away some of PepsiCo's best "Tigers," and they were, because of the constant pressure, willing to go. (PepsiCo's rate of tenure is less than one-third of the rate at Penney's.) And what, according to *Business Week*, was the major problem at Penney's? Lack of competitiveness. Despite a reputation as one of the best places to work, and despite intense employee and customer loyalty, Penney's had been rapidly losing market share to K Mart. Some critics expressed doubt that Penney's could respond to the challenge.

What is happening here? The surface conclusion is that two opposite cultures exist. Penney's reflects the human relations model in that the company seems to resemble a team, clan, or family. PepsiCo reflects the rational goal model in that it appears to be an instrumental firm. The strength of one is the weakness of the other. While this conclusion is true, there is a deeper insight to be gained. I will later return to this interesting contrast after considering the transformation of values.

Ineffectiveness

In the last chapter I presented the competing values framework, which consisted of juxtaposed sets of organizational effectiveness criteria. There, and in Chapter Three, I argued that each of these "good" criteria can become overvalued by an individual and pursued in a unidimensional fashion. When this zealous pursuit of a single set of criteria takes place, a strange inversion can also result. Good things can mysteriously become bad things. In Figure 9, I show how criteria of effectiveness, when pursued blindly, become criteria of ineffectiveness. These latter criteria are depicted in the negative zone on the outside of the diagram.

The structure of this model parallels the competing values framework of effectiveness. The axes, however, are negatively, rather than positively, labeled. Thus, the vertical dimension ranges from chaos (too much flexibility and spontaneity) to rigidity (too much order and predictability). The horizontal dimension ranges from belligerence and hostility (too much external focus and too much emphasis on competition and engagement) to apathy and indifference (too much internal focus and too much emphasis on maintenance and coordination within the system). Each quadrant represents a negative culture with negative effectiveness criteria. Embedded within these quadrants are eight criteria of ineffectiveness.

In the upper-left quadrant is the irresponsible country club. In this quadrant, human relations criteria are emphasized to the point of encouraging laxity and negligence. Discussion and participation, good in themselves, are carried to inappropriate lengths. Commitment, morale, and human development turn into extreme permissiveness and uncontrolled individualism. Here, administrators are concerned only with employees, to the exclusion of the task.

In the upper-right quadrant is the tumultuous anarchy. In

Figure 9. The Positive and Negative Zones.

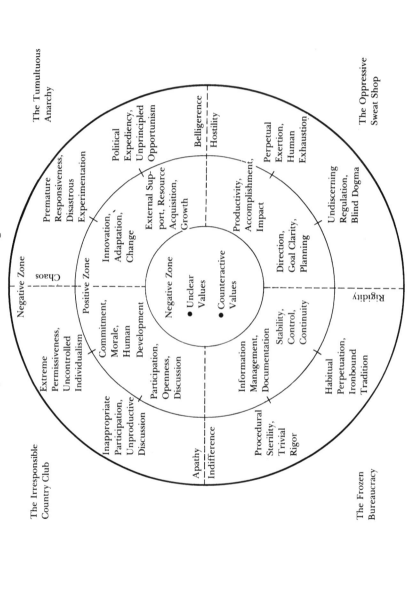

this quadrant, there is so much emphasis on the open systems criteria of effectiveness that disruption and discontinuity result. Emphasis on insight, innovation, and change turn into premature responsiveness and disastrous experimentation. Concern for external support, resource acquisition, and growth turn into political expediency and unprincipled opportunism. Here, administrators are concerned only with having a competitive advantage and show no interest in continuity and control of the work flow.

In the lower-right quadrant is the oppressive sweatshop. In this quadrant, there is too much emphasis on the criteria of effectiveness associated with the rational goal model. Effort, productivity, and emphasis on profit or impact of service turn into perpetual exertion and human exhaustion. Here, we see symptoms of burnout. Concern for goal clarification, authority, and decisiveness turn into an emphasis on strict regulation and blind dogma. There is no room for individual differences; the boss has the final say.

Finally, in the lower-left quadrant is the frozen bureaucracy. Here, there is too much concern with internal processes. The organization becomes atrophied as a result of excessive measurement and documentation; it becomes a system of red tape. Control measures, documentation, and computation turn into procedural sterility and trivial rigor. Everything is "by the book." The emphasis on stability, control, and continuity lead to the blind perpetuation of habits and traditions. Procedures are followed because "we've always done it this way"; there is no room for trying something new.

Strength Becoming Weakness

Let us return to PepsiCo and J. C. Penney. Earlier I said that introducing the culture of one company into the other would be highly conflictual. Further, I pointed out that each culture had weaknesses. Now we can see that their very strengths put them at risk.

Because of the inability of the PepsiCo culture to tolerate the values in the human resource quadrant, the company is in

danger of moving into the negative zone on the right side of
Figure 9. Because of the inability of the J. C. Penney culture to
more fully absorb the values on the right side of the figure, the
company is in danger of moving into the negative zone on the
left side of the figure. The more fully that each company pushes
a particular set of positive values, without tending to the opposite positive values, the greater the danger to it.

The major point here is that everything in the two outer
circles is related. The more that success is pursued around one
set of positive values, the greater will be the pressure to take into
account the opposite positive values. If these other values are
ignored long enough, crisis and catastrophe will result.

Organizations enter the internal negative zone when they
fail to establish a clear focus for themselves. Many organizations
have very unclear values or values that randomly counteract one
another. Indeed, this is frequently the case; very few organizations have a clearly focused set of values.

The Negative Zone as a Product of Individual Style

What produces out-of-balance cultures? How is the negative zone created? There are many answers to these questions,
but an important one is the individual bias, discussed in Chapter Three. To illustrate this, I will here contrast two very different
individuals, one who created and got trapped in a negative zone
and one who did not.

Don Burr of People Express. One of the most interesting management stories of this decade concerns Don Burr and how he used
his creative genius to build a spectacular company. But it is also a
story of how he turned his strengths into a problem, how he got
trapped in a negative zone, and how that led to the demise of the
company.

People Express was incorporated in April 1980. It was
driven by a unique vision. Among the key elements of this vision
were the ideas of offering extraordinarily inexpensive fares
made possible by large productivity gains, of focusing on the
high-density Eastern markets, and of operating out of the under-

utilized Newark International Airport. In a two-year period, the company grew to 1,200 employees, owned seventeen aircraft, was servicing thirteen cities, and had flown two million passengers. But this was just the beginning of the company's growth. Before its demise in 1986, People's would become the fifth largest airline in the country.

Before starting the company, Don Burr had been the president of Texas Air. When he left to start People Express, more than fifteen of Texas Air's top people followed him. At that time, although Burr was only thirty-nine years old, he was the oldest member of the new company. Many of the people who followed him left their old jobs knowing little or nothing about even the most basic aspects of the new company. They came because of their trust in Burr and the opportunity to build a new system.

From the beginning, the driving beliefs were that people were trustworthy and that this was a chance to build an organization where people could maximize their abilities. Burr's people were ingenious in creating the new company. They developed a unique vision based on low fares and convenient schedules. The company's aircraft were redesigned for the most efficient use and maximum carrying capacity. Hiring and training practices drew on unique labor pools, and employees developed a deep sense of commitment and teamwork. Labor costs were kept low by maintaining lean staffs who were highly motivated and willing to do any job deemed necessary. New ticketing and collection procedures were worked out. Technologies and administrative hierarchies were kept simple.

At the core of this were Burr's enthusiasm and entrepreneurial leadership. Never satisfied with a plateau, he continually pushed for more growth and greater effort and creativity on the part of the staff. Hackman (1984), for example, records a presentation that Burr made to his top people in October 1982:

> The spark in our organization went out sometime between last March and now. I've withdrawn, have been working less, and am less happy about it. I sense the same thing in others. This came to a

climax for me here two weeks ago in a meeting with Lori and Richard that was supposed to be about management development. We never even got to the issue. Instead, I spent most of the day complaining, pouring out my own anxiety. It was a good process for me. I learned a lot about me, about the company, and I've thought a lot about it since then.

I think I've come up with something. This is an entrepreneurial company, dedicated to growth and change. That's what we do best. When that ended, a piece of what we are ended with it. Sometime after March we switched from being a new venture to being an establishment company. People started going home to sleep. We lost the momentum. And we're not particularly good at maintenance. I know I'm not good at it; it doesn't engage me.

Do you share this view? If so, think about regunning the engines and doing more of what we set out to do three years ago. What we ought to do, given our present lethargy and the economic times, is set out on a new growth path, and get some aggressive plans in place.

We know how to do some things. We know how to do Part 121 [FAA certification]. We know how to market. We know how to buy airplanes. We know how to maintain them. But why muddle along doing what we know how to do? It's not reaching our potential. By next spring, we ought to be ready to make the next big push. What's to stop us? What are the constraints? Equipment? No. Money? No. Facilities? No. The FAA? No. The constraint is the people. But really that's not a constraint either. There are a thousand young people just like you already in the company, ready to go. And we can hire more. So our only real constraint is people who are knowledgeable and experienced enough to operate well in our kind of organization.

Communications. Supporting people. That's why our discussion today [the official agenda was to discuss implementation of the stucture package] is so important. The people process is our only real secret, the linchpin to our ability to move forward. It's the most important thing we have to do.

So we should set a new horizon, a bigger vision. If we are not excited, our people won't be either. We've got to rededicate ourselves to our people-oriented direction. We've lost track of it, and we have to get back with it because that is where our future is [Hackman, 1984, pp. 44–45 (used by permission)].

At the conclusion of the speech, Burr received a phone call indicating that it might be possible to open a new route to London. Were the managers ready for this new challenge, he asked? Their response was overwhelmingly positive.

Like the director of the mental health center leadership methods I discussed in the last chapter, Burr was clearly a very effective manager. Indeed, he has been one of the most creative managers of our time. But something went wrong. After five years of explosive growth his dream died. In September 1986, People Express was sold to its archrival, Texas Air. The death of People Express resulted in many post hoc analyses of what went wrong. Generally the analyses agreed on two themes. The first and most obvious theme concerned expansion, particularly People's well-publicized purchase of Frontier Airlines. Burr simply tried to expand the airline too rapidly.

The second theme had to do with the evolution of the company's infrastructure. Critics argued that Burr was unable to let the organization go through some necessary processes of formalization. They claimed that he failed to understand basic details, such as which routes were profitable and which were not. He was unable to let go of job rotation strategies, which were initially successful but eventually resulted in serious problems. He resisted the continually expressed need for more management and direction. The critics argued that Burr failed, in the end, because he had limited vision.

In the present context I would translate the statement to say that Don Burr, like the mental health administrator, could not balance competing values. He was a victim of his strengths. He was trapped by his own success. In the end, he was trapped in the negative zone.

Both Burr and the mental health administrator understood the first three phases of the transformational cycle set forth in Chapter Two. They understood how to create excellence, that is, they understood how to introduce challenge, how to get people to pursue a new vision and to experience synergy. But they did not understand the last phase of the cycle. They could not comprehend the necessity for equilibrium. This required a paradoxical understanding of organization and management.

Given the stories of Don Burr and of the mental health administrator, one might begin to conclude that entrepreneurial managers are doomed when the formalization crisis comes and that it is impossible for them to make the shift. But this is not true. Some managers are indeed able to master the competing demands of the transformational cycle. Let us turn to a successful case.

Bill Gates of Microsoft. Microsoft is the second largest software company in the world. Run by Bill Gates, who is still in his early thirties, Microsoft has been best known for its widely used MS DOS system. But in 1987 Gates was successful in convincing IBM to adopt its newest product, called Windows, for use in IBM's new line of personal computers. Upon completion of the agreement analysts began to predict that within twelve months Microsoft would become the largest software company in the world.

In many ways, Gates, like Burr, is the stereotypical entrepreneur. He is a technical genius with a burning mission. He feels a drive to bring the power of computing to the masses. His company is marked by considerable flexibility and excitement. The median age of the work force is thirty-one. People work long days, with Gates himself setting the example with an early morning to midnight routine. There are frequent picnics, programmers set their own hours, dress is casual, and the turnover rate is less than 10 percent.

The company has grown rapidly. From 1980 to 1981 Gates watched his company go from 80 to 125 employees and saw profits double to $16 million. The market value of the company now exceeds $2 billion. Given our earlier cases, all these indicators would lead us to worry about Gates and his ability to meet the demands for formalization.

In fact, however, Gates has already faced the formalization crisis and has come off well. What were the keys to this success? First, he made a very significant decision to bring in professional managers and to focus his own energies on technology. He seemed to grasp an important paradox that eludes most entrepreneurs: to have power means one must give up power. Maintaining a primary focus on technology, however, does not mean that he has abandoned the tasks of leadership. Instead, he has taken the time to learn the principles of law, marketing, distribution, and accounting and apply them in his work. He also has the paradoxical capacity of simultaneously caring and being tough. For example, dissatisfied with the performance of Microsoft's president, Gates removed him from office after only one year. But not long after, Gates was invited to be the best man at the wedding of the former president.

Staying in the Positive Zone

Perhaps the best summary of Gates and his abilities comes from one of his colleagues: "Bill Gates is very good at evaluating situations as they change." This, of course, is a key characteristic for staying in the positive zone.

Figure 9 has some important implications for management. It suggests that managers need to stay in the positive zone, that is, they need to pursue the seemingly "competing" positive values in the middle circle while also being careful to stay out of the external negative zone. They must maintain a dynamic, creative tension. Over time they must, like Bill Gates, be able to frame and reframe, that is, to move from one set of competing values to another. They must develop the skills and cognitive outlook that will allow them to become masters of management.

This is a radically different theory of management from those now current. It suggests that managers must continually change and balance opposites and that they must have a complex and dynamic theory of behavior. To pursue some single set of values, as implied in most of the existing theories of management, is both unrealistic and potentially dangerous. A master of management must be able to understand and work with deep change.

6

Competing Values
and the Dynamics
of Managerial Leadership

While organizations are often dynamic, complex, and contradictory, the capacity to see organizations as dynamic, complex, and contradictory does not come easily. In the preceding chapter a framework was presented to help you think about them in such a fashion. In this chapter the model is extended to the realm of managerial leadership.

A Primary Differentiation

In making sense of the world, people tend to favor one of two very different ways of thinking. The first is analytic, sequential, rational, time oriented, discontinuous, and verbal. The second is holistic, synthetic, visuospatial, intuitive, timeless, diffuse, and nonverbal. In recent theories the first way of thinking has been associated with the left hemisphere of the brain and the second with the right hemisphere. The left hemisphere, which is dominant during waking hours, processes language and is responsible for analytic thinking. The right hemisphere is dominant when we dream and is the source of holistic thinking.

There are, of course, many who question if the brain actually functions in this way. Whatever the empirical results come to eventually show about hemispheric information processing, we should note the conceptual power of the differentiation between the types of thinking. The differentiation occurs regularly. In reviewing a wide-ranging literature, from Homer to Chomsky, Hampden-Turner (1981) finds twenty-three major differentiations that basically reflect the two modes of thinking. In each case the two concepts reflect an opposition with strong moral overtones about how to engage in or think about social action. Clearly there is something very fundamental about the differentiation. While I am not fully convinced that the differentiation can be attributed to hemispheric information processes, I will occasionally use the terms *right-* and *left-brain thinking* for their metaphorical or heuristic value.

In the management literature this general differentiation, although not discussed in exactly the same terms, occurs with some regularity. Some examples are Barnard's (1938) logical and nonlogical processes, Gouldner's (1959) rational and natural systems, McGregor's (1960) Theory X and Theory Y, Zaleznik's (1977) manager and leader, and Burns's (1978) transactional and transformational leadership.

Perhaps the best known of these dichotomies is McGregor's (1960). He identified two orientations, Theory X and Theory Y. The first assumes that people are interested only in security and have little ambition or desire for responsibility. In order to get such people to put forth enough effort to achieve objectives, they must be coerced, controlled, directed, or threatened with punishment. The second theory assumes that people are willing to exercise self-direction and self-control in the pursuit of goals to which they are committed and for which they are rewarded. Here management involves a much more open and participative approach. While the first view is tied to equilibrium, structure, authority, and direction, the second is tied to change, adaptation, mutuality, and commitment. The first reflects a left-brain orientation and the second a right-brain orientation. (Again, I am using the two terms in a metaphorical sense.)

Most people find McGregor's differentiation to be very powerful in making sense of how people manage. Other differentiations often echo his. In *Stodgill's Handbook of Leadership* (Bass, 1981), for example, there are five chapters reviewing the extensive research on management style. Four of these are broken into dichotomies that clearly match McGregor's differentiation: democratic-autocratic; participative-directive; relations oriented-task oriented; and consideration-initiating structure. In each case the first style fits Theory Y and the second style Theory X.

While the labels change, the basic differentiation seems to occur over and over. A good example is Zaleznik's (1977) differentiation between managers and leaders. He argues that managers are conservators and regulators in that their sense of self-worth comes from perpetuating existing institutions and their role is built around duty and responsibility. In contrast, leaders do not "belong" to the organization, and their object is to "profoundly alter human, economic, and political relationships" (p. 76). While managers have a passive orientation toward goals, leaders try to shape and influence them. While managers act to limit choices, leaders seek to develop new alternatives and new approaches. While the relationships of managers with people have low emotional content, the relationships leaders have with people are rich in emotional content.

The Zaleznik article brought numerous responses from readers. Among them were letters from a number of chief executive officers. One theme in the letters that took issue with the article was that people have to be both leaders and managers and that Zaleznik's differentiation between them, while it may have some validity, is too exaggerated.

This point about exaggeration is very important because as people move higher in organizations they are more likely to face the problem of needing to both manage and lead, to be both people and task focused, to meet the assumptions on both sides of the above differentiations. But while we may often need to employ both sets of assumptions, most of us are schismogenic. We see the world from a right- or left-brain perspective. Hence, we think that one view is correct and the other incorrect. We espouse Theory X and reject Theory Y or vice versa. We accept the need for management and reject the need for leadership or vice versa. It is very difficult to simultaneously conceive of both orientations as positive and desirable. While real situations demand that we do just this, our personal orientations and most formal theories lead us to value one approach over the other.

An interesting example is provided by Burns (1978), who clearly differentiated transactional leadership from transformational leadership. Transactional leaders are like Zaleznik's managers in that they are instrumentally oriented. Their relationships are based on exchange. They know what people want from their work, and they see that they get the desired rewards when performance is up to standards. Transformational leaders are very different. They raise the awareness of others, they inspire people to transcend their self-interests for the sake of the larger collectivity, and they stimulate the higher-level needs that people might have. In another important book, which built on the work of Burns, Bass (1985) makes the following observation about one of his few differences with Burns: "He sees transformational leadership as the opposite end of a single continuum from transactional leadership. Conceptually and empirically, we find that leaders will exhibit a variety of patterns of transformational and transactional leadership. Most leaders do both but in different amounts" (p. 22). What is needed is a tool that explicitly helps us to avoid making either/or differentiations. It is for this purpose that we turn to the competing values model of managerial leadership.

Competing Values Model

Earlier I introduced the four models in the competing values framework and explored them at the organizational level. Here I will develop them at the managerial level. Each model or set of assumptions is shown in Table 1. The first two columns are consistent with left-brain or Theory X assumptions while the latter two are consistent with right-brain or Theory Y assumptions.

In the rational goal model people are assumed to have a high need for achievement. The primary information-processing style is rational (see Chapter Three). Decision making is based on logic and is seen as decisive and final. The manager uses the legitimate power of his or her position, and

Table 1. Assumptions of Managerial Leadership.

	Left-Brain, Theory X Perspectives		Right-Brain, Theory Y Perspectives	
	Rational Goal Model	*Internal Process Model*	*Open Systems Model*	*Human Relations Model*
Motivation	Achievement	Security	Growth	Affiliation
Information Processing	Rational	Hierarchical	Developmental	Consensual
Decision Making	Logic Decisiveness	Documentation Accountability	Creativity External Legitimacy	Participation Support
Power and Influence	Legitimate Power Goal Clarification	Expert Power Information Control	Reward Power Resource Allocation	Relational Power Group Values
Leadership Style	Directive Goal Oriented	Conservative Cautious	Inventive Risk Taking	Concerned Supportive
Managerial Roles	Director Producer	Monitor Coordinator	Innovator Broker	Facilitator Mentor
Behaviors	Provides Structure Initiates Action	Provides Information Maintains Structure	Envisions Change Acquires Resources	Shows Concern Facilitates
Prime Function	Directing	Coordinating	Boundary Spanning	Relating
Organizational Form	Firm	Hierarchy	Adhocracy	Team
Effectiveness Values	Productivity Accomplishment	Stability Control	Growth Resource Acquisition	Value of Human Resource

tries to influence subordinates through goal clarification and rational persuasion. The leadership style is directive and goal or task oriented. The manager provides structure and initiates action, and his or her primary management function is to give direction. The form in which all this is assumed to occur is the firm, and the primary values are productivity and accomplishment.

In contrast, consider the assumptions in the human relations model. Here people are assumed to have a high need for affiliation. Information processing follows the consensual model (Chapter Three), and decision making is characterized by participation that is assumed to result in support. This manager's power is based on relationships, and he or she uses group values to influence people. The leadership style is concerned and supportive, and the primary roles are those of facilitator and mentor. In these roles the manager shows concern and facilitates interaction. His or her primary function is relating to people. These behaviors are assumed to take place in a team or clan setting, and the primary effectiveness criterion is the value of human resources.

In the internal process model people are assumed to have a high need for security, and the manager is a hierarchical information processor. Decision making is characterized by the fact that documentation is assumed to result in accountability. Power is based on expertise and influence on information control. The leadership style is conservative and cautious, and the primary roles are those of monitor and coordinator. Here the manager provides information and maintains structure. This coordinating function occurs in a hierarchy, and the key effectiveness values are assumed to be stability and control.

In contrast to the internal process model, we have the open systems model that assumes that people have a high need for growth, development, and stimulation. Information processing is reflected in the developmental approach (see Chapter Three), and decision making is characterized by flexibility, creativity, and external legitimacy. Power and influence are assumed to follow the capacity to acquire, control, and allocate resources or rewards. The leadership style is inventive and includes risk taking. The primary roles are those of innovator and broker, and the primary function is boundary spanning. All these are assumed to take place in an adhocracy where the major effectiveness values are growth and resource acquisition.

In Table 1 the four sets of assumptions appear to be very separate and distinct. In Figures 10 and 11 I show some of the assumptions in the format used in the last chapter. The first figure shows the four models. Around the outer portion of the diagram are eight leadership styles, and around the inner portion of the diagram are eight roles that leaders can play. The roles were more fully defined in Chapter Three. The axes are the same as those presented in the last chapter. In Figure 11 the same form is used to convey the relationships around assumptions of power and influence. (For an explanation of the literature upon which these two figures are based, see Quinn, 1984.)

Theoretical Advantages

The competing values framework offers some advantages for thinking about management. It makes perceptual biases clear, it makes values explicit, and it provides a dynamic focus. Finally, the elements of the framework are consistent with existing theoretical categories, and it allows us to move from a traditional, schismogenic, either/or approach to a both/and approach, thus making it possible for us to see management behavior in genuinely new ways.

Clarifying Perceptual Bias. The framework makes clear that there are perceptual biases that influence how we see social action. These are reflected in the oppositional nature of the framework. Any point on one side of the diagram is in perceptual tension with any point on the opposite side of the diagram. The elements are not opposites in a mutually exclusive sense like short and tall. Empirically, it is possible to engage in behaviors at two opposite points in the framework. It is possible, for example, to play both the innovator and coordinator roles or both the producer and facilitator roles. Perceptually, however, we see these as very different behaviors, and we often treat them

Figure 10. Competing Values Framework of Leadership Roles.

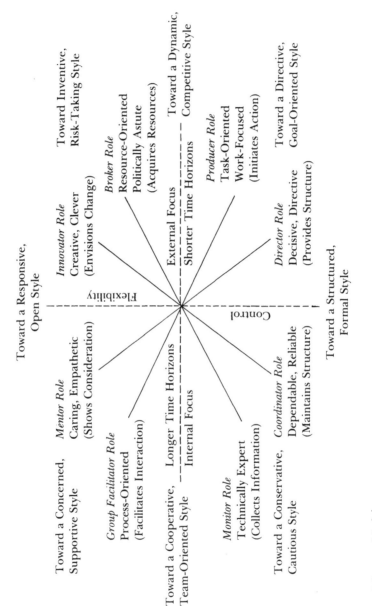

Human Relations Model

Open Systems Model

Internal Process Model

Rational Goal Model

Toward a Responsive, Open Style

Toward a Concerned, Supportive Style

Mentor Role
Caring, Empathetic
(Shows Consideration)

Group Facilitator Role
Process-Oriented
(Facilitates Interaction)

Toward a Cooperative, Team-Oriented Style

Longer Time Horizons
Internal Focus

Monitor Role
Technically Expert
(Collects Information)

Toward a Conservative, Cautious Style

Coordinator Role
Dependable, Reliable
(Maintains Structure)

Flexibility

Control

Innovator Role
Creative, Clever
(Envisions Change)

Toward Inventive, Risk-Taking Style

Broker Role
Resource-Oriented
Politically Astute
(Acquires Resources)

Toward a Dynamic, Competitive Style

External Focus
Shorter Time Horizons

Producer Role
Task-Oriented
Work-Focused
(Initiates Action)

Toward a Directive, Goal-Oriented Style

Director Role
Decisive, Directive
(Provides Structure)

Toward a Structured, Formal Style

Figure 11. Competing Values Framework of Power and Influence.

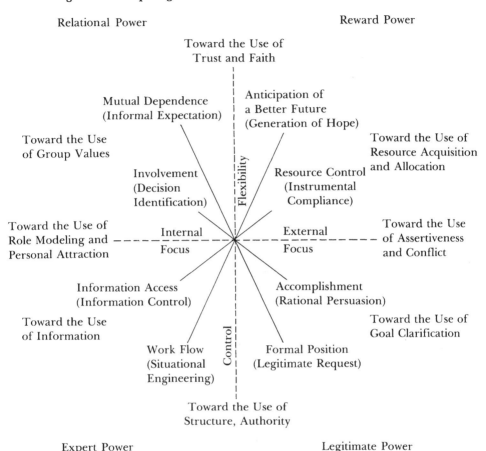

in a schismogenic way. That is, we see one as desirable and the other as not, or we concentrate on one and ignore the other entirely.

Making Values Explicit. Because each element is juxtaposed with its opposite, its meaning is made even clearer than it usually would be and the values surrounding both elements are made more explicit. This is true at each level of differentiation, in each half of the framework. In each quadrant and in each element the underlying values are clear and are positively presented. Hence, in the framework there is no assumed right answer, no one best way to manage. As an assessment tool, the framework does not impose values. It makes explicit those values that most assessors carry around implicitly and ensures that other values are also considered in a positive way.

Dynamic Focus. Because the explicit values are competing in a cognitive sense, the framework is tension bound. Just as organizations are usually not without tension, neither are managers. There are no clear maps for problem detection and solution. Many diverse kinds of behaviors are expected, and these are, at minimum, distant, at maximum, competing. The framework allows for the dynamic tensions that can sometimes be at the heart of managerial life. It also allows for the fact that behaviors may change. A manager may engage in a set of behaviors reflecting one set of values at one point and in an entirely different set of values at another point.

Consistent with Existing Categories. The general relationship of the above roles to existing theory can be seen in Table 2. The factors, categories, and observational systems of two well-known approaches are placed next to those roles that they most closely approximate. For illustrative purposes, a maximum of two entries are provided for each role from each author. In some cases labels are slightly misleading, but categorization is based on all items in a factor or description. The major point is that the framework is consistent with existing categories in the literature.

From Either/or to Both/and Thinking. Because the categories are not mutually exclusive, it is possible to locate behaviors outside our predetermined frames. Consider the either/or assumptions built into McGregor's Theory X and Theory Y. If we observe a real manager from this frame, we will have to conclude that the person belongs to one or the other category. Using the competing values approach, however, we may decide that the person belongs neither to X nor to Y. This would happen when the

Table 2. A Comparison of the Eight Role Categories
with Other Approaches.

Roles in This Study	Luthans and Lockwood (1984)	Yukl (1981)
1. Producer Role		• Performance Emphasis • Inspiration
2. Director Role	• Planning/Coordination	• Goal Setting • Role Clarification
3. Coordinator	• Decision Making/ Problem Solving • Disciplining/Punishing	• Coordinating • Problem Solving

4. Monitor Role	• Processing Paper Work
	• Monitoring/Controlling
	  Performance
		• Information
		  Dissemination
		• Internal Monitoring

5. Facilitator Role	• Managing Conflict	• Interaction Facilitation • Conflict Management
6. Mentor Role	• Motivating/Reinforcing • Training/Developing	• Consideration • Praise Recognition
7. Innovator Role		
8. Broker Role	• Interacting with Outsiders • Socializing/Politicking	• Representation • External Monitoring

person has high scores along the horizontal rather than the vertical axis. The person may turn out to be both X and Y. This would happen when scores are high on all the axes.

While this point may seem unimportant, it is not. It implies a radically different approach to measurement with very different implications in terms of what we tell people about their management style. Consider, for example, the well-known Myers-Briggs test (Myers, 1962) that reflects many of the assumptions in the present framework but is measured in an either/or fashion. The results are that a person comes out reflecting only one of the four quadrants. While the test is helpful for some purposes, it is not as realistic as it could be.

This last advantage, the capacity to go beyond existing frames, becomes very important as we turn to the central focus of the next chapter. There we ask how ineffective managers differ from one another in terms of their role patterns, and we ask the same question about effective managers. Using the model set forth in this chapter, we will be able to identify master managers and how they differ from others.

7

Profiles of Effective
and Ineffective Managers

In Chapter Four it was argued that the manager's role is to balance a set of contradictory positive values and to avoid the blind pursuit of any one value so as not to become trapped in a negative zone. Masters of management have the capacity to read many different kinds of cues, to form temporary strategies tied to the most important cues, and then to develop new strategies as other cues begin to emerge.

To fully engage the world in this fashion, a master manager must be able to transcend style. This means getting free of his or her preferred way of seeing and behaving. In fact, it often means seeing the world in a way that is the opposite of the way he or she prefers to see it. This, of course, is not easy to do. But fortunately, as we will learn in this chapter, you do not have to become a master manager to be an effective manager. While some people are blinded by their styles and become ineffective, others work well within their styles and are quite effective. There are, however, a few who transcend style and become masters.

In this chapter we will attempt to more fully understand the performance of those who are ineffective, those who are effective, and those who are the masters. I will begin by reviewing the two most commonly differentiated styles of managing. I will then use the competing values model, as explained in Chapter Six, to integrate these two perspectives. This integration will then guide an empirical examination of ineffective and effective behaviors. This analysis will reveal some archetypes of managerial performance, and I will discuss the implications of these archetypes. In Chapter Nine you will find the materials necessary to construct a profile of your own.

A Study of Archetypes

Here I will review a study done by Quinn, Faerman, and Dixit (1987). In the study 295 people were asked to describe the manager they knew best. These respondents were part-time M.B.A. and M.P.A. students from ten different universities in the United States. To describe the manager, they were given an instrument measuring each of the roles on the competing values framework. The 295 respondents were broken down into two samples, so that the roles could be measured in two different ways on two different questionnaires. One hundred and eighty-one people comprised the primary sample and 114 the secondary sample. In the analysis it was possible to compare the data generated by these two different approaches in order to see if similar results were obtained.

The first step in the study was to examine role performance by hierarchical level for the entire sample in order to determine how much emphasis is put on each role at each level of management. In other words, we wanted to determine whether role profiles change from level to level.

The results can be seen in Figures 12 and 13. Figure 12 contains the four diagrams for the four roles at the bottom of the framework. The scores on each role are found on the vertical axis to the left. The higher the score, the more emphasis that is placed on the role by the manager who is being described. On the horizontal axis are five levels of management. The data are analyzed for significant differences from level to level. When significant differences do occur, they are indicated by a bracket with a star. The only significant difference that occurs in Figure 12, however, is associated with the producer role. There is a significant difference between first-line supervision and each of the other levels of management. At all four levels managers are perceived to put more emphasis on the producer role than do first-line supervisors. Hence, on the bottom four roles in the framework, there is little difference from one management level to the next.

The patterns are very different for the top four roles, which show much more variation from level to level. Emphasis on the facilitator role drops off at the middle-management level and then takes a statistically significant jump at the upper-middle level. The change in the mentor role is more dramatic still. Here the emphasis falls off significantly as the focus moves to the middle level but it then increases significantly in the upper-middle and top levels. The innovator and broker roles show a steady increase as the focus moves to successively higher levels, with a more dramatic incline for the broker role.

The results suggest that, for the most part, the emphasis changes very little on the bottom four roles. With the exception of first-line supervisors, most managers put fairly high emphasis on the producer role, and this does not change as the focus moves up. Emphasis on director, coordinator, and monitor roles also tends to remain steady. The two roles in the human relations quadrant—those of facilitator and mentor—drop off as the focus moves to middle management, but they then climb significantly. The innovator and broker roles increase steadily as the focus moves up.

These patterns tend to confirm earlier discussions. Recall the story of the engineer in Chapter One. He excelled at the rational thinking associated with the bottom roles and did well in his early years. But at higher levels he suddenly found himself in difficulty because he did not value the assumptions underlying the human relations and open systems quadrants. To him, political considerations and demands for discussion were "not real." It took a major shift in his world view for him even to begin to play the roles at the top of the framework. The data in our study suggest that his situation was not an isolated one. As people move up in an organization, the emphasis on the top four roles tends to increase. People need a more dynamic and complex world view in order to cope with the complexity and change that are encountered at higher levels.

Figure 12. Performance by Management Level: Bottom Four Roles.

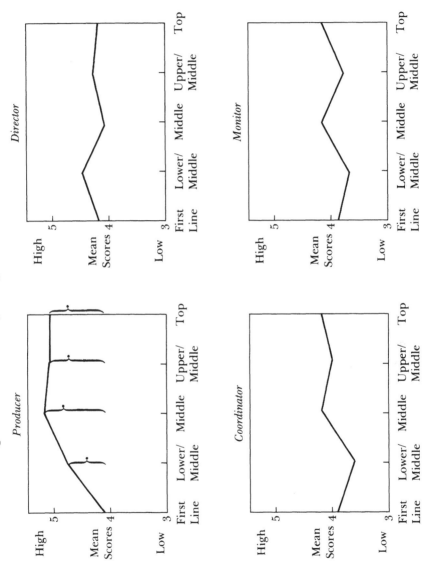

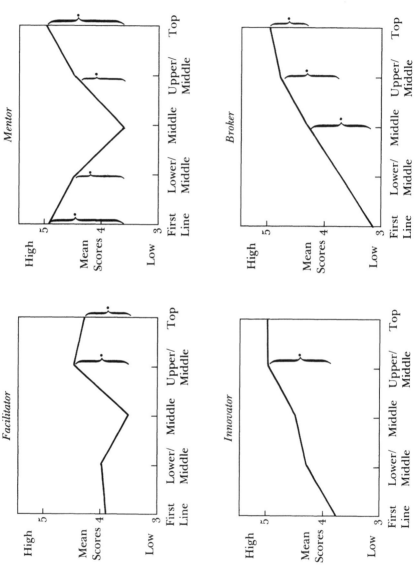

Figure 13. Performance by Management Level: Top Four Roles.

Exploring for Archetypes

The central question in the study had to do with performance. In organizations some managers are perceived as highly effective, others as highly ineffective. We wanted to know more about the people who were perceived in either of these ways. Our question was, How do managers with highly positive images differ from one another? Are there some archetypes of effective performance? Likewise, are there archetypes of ineffective performance?

There are two unusual aspects to this approach. First of all, generalized perceptions of performance are normally seen as halo, a form of error. The general values of respondents are thought to distort their objectivity in reporting the behaviors that social scientists want to understand. Because of this orientation, generalized perception is seen as a variable to be controlled rather than as an important dependent variable. As some researchers have pointed out, however, perceived overall effectiveness is a very important real world factor (Turner, 1960; Landy, Barnes-Farell, Vance, and Steel, 1980). Positive or negative perception determines what happens to managers, and managers are concerned with creating and maintaining a positive image. From those who are successful and those who are unsuccessful, what can we learn?

Second, the analytic question is here couched in a different way from that found in most studies. Normally, if we are trying to study a dependent variable such as perceived effectiveness, we attempt to predict it by using independent variables — in this case, we would use the measures of the eight roles. Such an analysis would result in a generalized statement about the overall group. We might learn, for example, that perceived effectiveness is a function of emphasis on the director and innovator roles. We would then conclude that to be perceived as effective a manager needs to emphasize these two areas. The competing values framework, however, leads us to suspect such a conclusion. Is it not possible to make trade-offs? Are some people able to defy the general trend and still be seen as effective? Here we want to know how the people who are perceived as effective or ineffective differ from one another. We are looking for patterns of emphasis across the roles or for archetypes of effectiveness and ineffectiveness.

In doing the analysis, we separated out people who scored very high or very low on perceived overall effectiveness. These two groups of high and low performers became the focus of our analysis. Because we wanted to explore differences between the high performers and differences between the low performers, I used a technique called *cluster analysis*. I clustered together the people who had similar patterns of emphasis on the eight roles in the competing values framework. This served to identify people with similar approaches. We then computed a profile for each of these groups, and following that we compared the groups on the basis of demographic variables and qualitative statements written by the respondents. This allowed us to identify some tentative archetypes of effective and ineffective managers.

In the last sentence I use the word *tentative* because this is an initial exploratory study. It has many limitations that remain to be addressed in the future. I see the results as hypotheses or the basis for a new theory rather than as final conclusions. Despite this tentative quality, the findings illustrate a new way to think about effective and ineffective performance.

The Findings: Ineffectives

The analysis of the low-scoring group resulted in the emergence of seven archetypes of ineffective management (Figure 14). The profiles are plotted as standard scores and compared to the scores for the entire sample. The zero or middle line in the diagram represents the 50th percentile for the whole sample. The line marked 1 means one standard deviation or the 84th percentile. The line marked 2 means two standard deviations or the 98th percentile for the whole sample. Minus one is the 16th percentile and minus two the 2nd percentile.

Chaotic Adaptives. The first cluster consists of people who are above the overall sample mean for the top four roles and who are below the mean for the bottom four roles. They score quite low on the coordinator role. In the qualitative comments they are described as individuals who short-cut administrative processes, who are not involved in details, who are uninterested in planning, and who look for quick fixes. Demographically, they tend to be in upper-middle management positions, but, surprisingly enough, they tend to have only high school educations. While their abilities in the upper two quadrants may have helped them to move up without the benefit of much formal education, their shortcomings in the lower roles, particularly the lower-left roles, may have now caught up with them in that they are seen as ineffective in these roles.

Abrasive Coordinators. The people in this cluster are almost the opposite of those in the first cluster in that they are above the mean on three of the lower roles and below the mean on the rest. They are particularly weak on the top four. Qualitatively they are described as conservative, rigid people with closed minds who demand conformity. This cluster is made up entirely of males who have considerable graduate training and who are found only in middle and lower-middle levels of management. The strengths of the abrasive coordinators, in the lower-left three roles, apparently do not make up for their deficiencies in the other roles, particularly in dealing with people and with change, and they are hence seen as ineffective managers.

Drowning Workaholics. The people in this cluster approach the overall sample mean only on the producer role. They are particularly low on the facilitator, mentor, innovator, broker, and director roles. These people are described as obsessive about work, overly sensitive to criticism, unable to delegate authority, bogged down in detail, and overly formal in relating to subordinates. This pattern occurs at all levels of management; of the ineffective clusters, it is the one in which females occur most frequently (36 percent). These managers are seen as ineffective because they believe they must do all the work themselves and because they are limited in their abilities to direct or work with other people.

Figure 14. Profiles of Perceived Ineffectiveness.

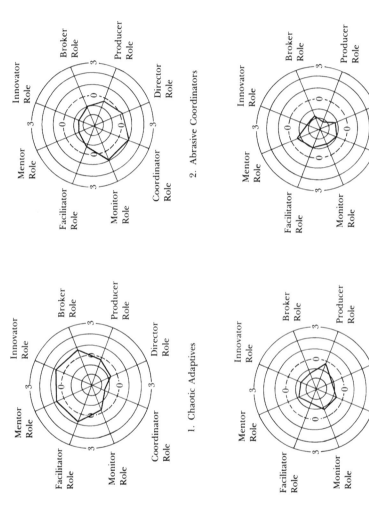

1. Chaotic Adaptives

2. Abrasive Coordinators

3. Drowning Workaholics

4. Extreme Unproductives

Figure 14, Cont'd.

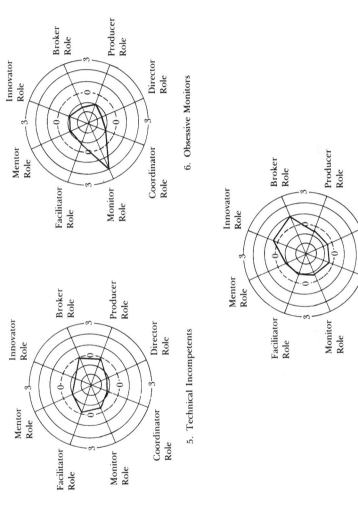

5. Technical Incompetents

6. Obsessive Monitors

7. Disorganized Externals

Extreme Unproductives. The people in this cluster have low scores on all the roles. They are below the second standard deviation on each of the four roles to the right of the figure, and they are particularly characterized by their low performance in the producer role. These people are seen as unproductive and uncommitted to their work role. They are also seen as defensive in responding to questions or challenges and are said to snap at people, give quick answers, or insist on having the final word. The people in this cluster tend to be in first-line or lower-middle management positions (70 percent). This group scores lower than any other on perceived effectiveness and stimulates more intense negative comments than any other.

Technical Incompetents. Although they approach the mean on the broker and producer roles, the people in this cluster score low on the top and bottom two roles. They provide little direction or coordination, nor do they show much interest in people or new ideas. They are described as externally rather than internally focused. They are seen as unreliable, unpredictable, and uninvolved. These people tend to be in middle and upper-middle management positions; they are seen as ineffective because they focus only on external issues such as marketing or politics and show little competence or technical skill in managing their units.

Obsessive Monitors. The people in this cluster score low on all roles but one. They are extremely high on the monitor role. These people are seen as intolerant and as slaves to detail. The people in this cluster tend to be males. None are in upper-middle or top management positions. They are seen as ineffective because they are obsessively concerned with details while doing poorly on most other dimensions.

Disorganized Externals. The people in this cluster are above the mean on the two roles to the upper right of the diagram. They are nearly a full standard deviation above the mean on the broker role. They fall below the mean on the director, coordinator, monitor, facilitator, and mentor roles. These people are described as disorganized and permissive. They tend to be in upper- and top-level positions, and are seen as ineffective because they are sloppy with details and overly permissive with people.

The Findings: Effectives

The analysis of the group with high scores on perceived overall effectiveness resulted in the emergence of six clusters. These appear in Figure 15. As in the preceding section, the clusters are conveyed in standard scores and are compared to the overall sample mean.

Conceptual Producers. The nine people in the first cluster of effectives are approximately a standard deviation above the mean on six of the roles. On the coordinator role, however, they fall to the mean, and on the monitor role they fall a full standard deviation below the mean. In the qualitative statements, these people are seen as conceptually skilled in that they work well with ideas. They seem to be particularly good at coming up with and selling new ideas. Seemingly consistent with this is the fact that these people have a much higher level of graduate education (78 percent) than do the people in the other effective clusters. For the most part they are in the upper-middle levels of management. These people, then, tend to be highly trained, conceptually skilled, production-oriented managers who pay relatively little attention to details but who are seen as clearly effective.

Aggressive Achievers. The people in this cluster score high on the four bottom roles and also show some strength in the innovator role. They are at or below the mean on the remaining roles. They are particularly low on the facilitator role. They are seen as having extensive technical knowledge and coordinative skills but are also seen as being somewhat insensitive and bureaucratic. Interestingly, everyone in this cluster is in middle management, and it is the only cluster of effective people that has no females.

Figure 15. Profiles of Perceived Effectives.

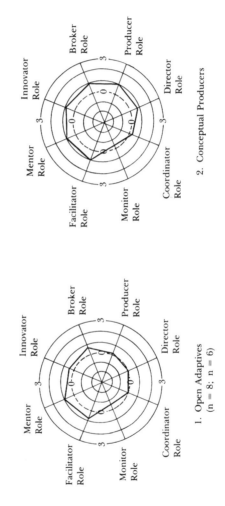

1. Open Adaptives
   (n = 8; n = 6)

2. Conceptual Producers

Figure 15, Cont'd.

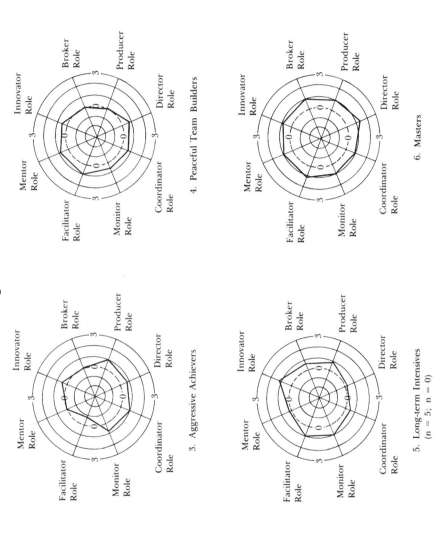

3. Aggressive Achievers

4. Peaceful Team Builders

5. Long-term Intensives
(n = 5; n = 0)

6. Masters

Peaceful Team Builders. While above the mean on six of the roles, this group is near the mean on the broker and producer roles. From the qualitative statements comes the perception of a person who does not become rattled under pressure and who is good at managing conflict and making people feel part of a collective effort. This cluster has the second highest percentage of people in upper-middle and top management positions (67 percent) and the second highest percentage of people with graduate educations (67 percent). Here are upper-level, well-trained people, who remain calm in a crisis and who are seen as highly effective.

Committed Intensives. The people in this cluster have a highly varied profile. They are high on the innovator, producer, monitor, and facilitator roles and fall near the mean on the mentor, director, and coordinator roles. In each quadrant they have a high and an average role. They are characterized by the high intensity that they bring to their work. They are almost obsessive about personal industry for themselves and for others, to the point that they may have difficulty understanding individuals who are not willing to work as hard as they are. These are primarily middle and upper-middle managers.

Open Adaptives. The highest scores for this group are on the top four roles. In the other roles they tend to fall near the mean, with the exception of the monitor role, where they fall a standard deviation below the mean. In the qualitative statements these people are portrayed as being very open, reasonable, and easy-going, while also having a tendency to be too permissive with their subordinates. This pattern of effective management tends to emerge at the lower (57 percent) and upper (43 percent) levels rather than in the middle.

Masters. The fifteen people in this cluster are approximately a standard deviation higher than the mean on all eight roles. Qualitative descriptions of these people are glowing statements that indicate that they are seen as superb managerial leaders. Nevertheless, every individual in the group is seen, by the respondents, to have some weakness. There appear to be no consistent themes in these weaknesses. That is, while no one of these high performers is perfect, there is no one weakness that is common to all of them. Three-fourths of the people in this cluster are in upper-middle and top management positions. While two-thirds of the people in the cluster are males, more of the women who are perceived as effective appear in this cluster than any other (46 percent of the effective females). These people are seen as highly effective because they play all the roles. They seem to have overcome their blind spots and in the process to have become masters of management.

Implications of the Findings

While the findings have some interesting implications, they remain hypotheses in need of further exploration rather than facts that have been demonstrated in any final sense. Here I will discuss some of the implications of these hypotheses.

The Need for Balance. The ineffective profiles seem to fall into two groups. There are those who do poorly on nearly all the roles and those who exceed the mean on three or four roles. In the first group are the drowning workaholics, extreme unproductives, technical incompetents, and obsessive monitors. In the second group are the chaotic adaptives, abrasive coordinators, and disorganized externals. While the first are easy to classify as ineffective, the profiles in the second group are more complex. They appear to be both good and bad.

Given that they are doing well on some roles, why are these groups seen as ineffective rather than effective? The issue seems to be one of balance. For the ineffective groups, the positive scores simply do not counterbalance the negative. This can perhaps best be seen by comparing the profile of the abrasive coordinators, who are seen as ineffective, with the profile of the aggressive achievers, who are seen as effective. The shapes of the two profiles are very similar, because both put emphasis on the bottom rather than the top roles. The difference between the profiles is thus found not so much in their shape as in their size.

The aggressive achievers have a much larger profile, and the abrasive coordinators score considerably lower on all roles but two. It would seem that the profiles in the second group—those with high scores on some roles—are seen as ineffective because they are so far out of balance. Managers cannot achieve effectiveness by emphasizing two or three roles while ignoring the others.

The qualitative statements about the chaotic adaptives, abrasive coordinators, and disorganized externals provide another interesting insight. In the statements describing these people, a perceptual transformation seems to occur. The highest scores in these profiles are not necessarily seen as strengths. They are redefined as weaknesses. The chaotic adaptives, for example, score above the mean on the top four roles. They seemingly emphasize people, change, and politics, yet they are described as people who go around causing chaos. Thus, their highest scores are seen not as indicators of strength but of weakness. They are not seen as innovative but as unpredictable and disruptive. A similar phenomenon occurs with the other two profiles.

Imbalance and Vicious Circles. It may be that when people underplay a number of roles the effort that they put into their preferred roles becomes negatively defined by those around them. Perhaps effectiveness is the result of maintaining a creative tension between contrasting demands in a social system. When the tension is lost, the perception of effectiveness is altered. The roles that are emphasized are seen negatively. A perceptual inversion occurs.

Theoretically, the notion of a seemingly positive characteristic being perceptually inverted is intriguing. It ties into the notion of schismogenesis, perceptual splits (Klein, 1959), and strange loops (Hofstadter, 1979). All these suggest that when a value in the realm of social action is ideologically split off from its opposite and pursued in an obsessive fashion, some kind of strange loop or inversion may take place (Hampden-Turner, 1981). Systems begin to lose necessary positive tensions, often entering into vicious circles of decreasing effectiveness (Masuch,

Figure 16. Organizational Levels of Ineffective Archetypes.

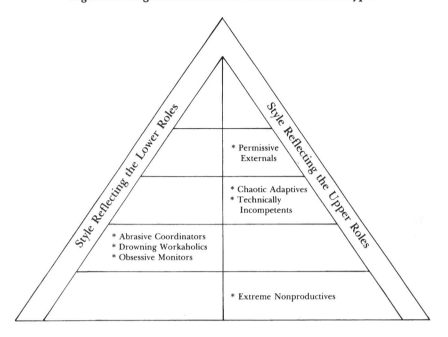

1985). When this occurs, people often increase their commitment to the value that is already being overemphasized. This
frequently has catastrophic outcomes.

Style and Effectiveness. It appears, however, that one does not
have to emphasize all the roles in order to be seen as effective.
The conceptual producers and open adaptives both fall well
below the mean on the monitor role but are seen as effective. As
noted above, the aggressive achievers fall below the mean on
three roles but are still seen as effective. Taken collectively, the
six effective patterns suggest that one can put average or even
below-average emphasis on one or two roles and still be seen as
effective. Even though these people have weaknesses, they maintain enough balance and creative tension to be seen as effective.

Style and the Evolution of Mastery. This chapter began with a
discussion of information processing and styles of behavior. It

Figure 17. Organizational Levels of Effective Archetypes.

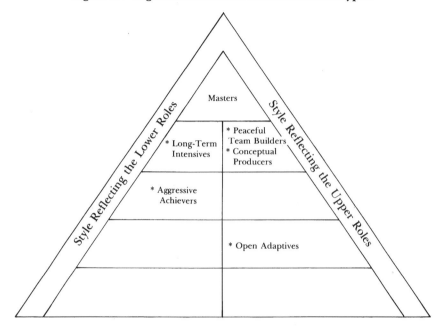

pointed out the tendency to differentiate between right-brain and left-brain thinking or Theory Y and Theory X assumptions in making sense of management. People who follow right-brain or Theory Y assumptions emphasize the top four roles in the framework, while people who make left-brain or Theory X assumptions emphasize the bottom four roles. Given the pervasiveness of this differentiation, it is interesting to review the profiles in terms of style. Do the profiles reflect these styles? Is one style more effective than another? Do any profiles transcend style?

The profiles do tend to reflect the role differentiation mentioned above. As seen in Figures 16 and 17, twelve of the thirteen profiles can be classified into one category or the other. These figures reflect both style (on either side of the middle line) and management level (first-line supervision at the bottom and top management at the top). Notice that both the effective and the ineffective profiles can be categorized. One can have a right-brain, Theory Y approach and be seen as either effective or ineffective. Similarly, one can have a left-brain, Theory X approach and be either effective or ineffective.

There is only one profile that seems to transcend style, namely, the cluster we have labeled masters. These people have high scores on all eight roles. Collectively, they are at higher levels of management than are those in other profiles, they have been in the organization longer than others, and they have a large female representation.

Apparently these people are not blocked by a blind spot. They are able to think and behave in a variety of ways. It is important that these people tend to appear at higher levels of management because it suggests that they were not born as masters. They evolved. Earlier they must have had some other profile, but they gradually learned to enlarge it. I will return to this particular point in the next chapter.

8

The Road to Mastery: An Agenda for Transforming Your Management Style

"A good sense of relevance and timing is often treated as though it were a 'Gift' or 'Intuition' rather than something that can be learned, something spontaneous rather than something planned. The opposite is nearer the truth. One is more likely to 'capture the moment' when everything one has learned is readily available. . . . Perhaps it is our training in linear cause-and-effect thinking and the neglect of our capacities for imagery that makes us so often unable to see the multiple potential of the moment. Entering the situation 'blank' is not the answer. One needs to have as many frameworks for seeing and strategies for acting available as possible. But it is not enough to involve only one's head in the situation: One's heart has to get involved too. Cornelia Otis Skinner once said that the first law of the stage is to love your audience. You can love your audience only if you love yourself. If you have relatively full access to your organized experience, to yourself, and to the situation, you will capture the moment more often" (Shepard, 1983, p. 426).

The critical point in this statement is that a good sense of relevance and timing, or the ability to capture the moment, comes from having as many frameworks and strategies as possible. Because each quadrant in the competing values framework represents a different strategic frame, a person with a weak quadrant is less able to "capture the moment" than a master who can see and act from all four quadrants. Mastery is an evolution-

110

ary phenomenon, and the journey from novice to master involves a learning process.

There are at least two kinds of learning. The first involves an increment of improvement in an area or quadrant in which a person is already strong. The second involves work in a quadrant where a person is weaker. It is here that new frames are sometimes developed. It is here that one can sometimes make a discontinuous leap in one's capacity to "capture the moment." These leaps are often seen as transformations.

Sometimes individuals go through transformations in a spontaneous way. At other times, transformations are the result of conscious self-examination. In either case they involve considerable challenge and effort. Here I will review each of these two types and then present a step-by-step agenda for self-improvement.

Spontaneous Transformations

Developing a new frame or going through a transformation in style usually involves considerable discomfort. Consider, for example, the story of the engineer in Chapter One. He was a classic aggressive achiever who had risen quickly in the hierarchy. But upon entering the realm of upper management, he found himself at a loss. His hierarchical models and hard-edged strategies were no longer working. Notions of participation and political processes, often required at those levels, were antithetical to all that he believed in. He had no appropriate frame that allowed him to "capture the moment." The more he pushed his past strategies, the worse things became. He went through considerable pain for several years. During this time his underlying assumptions, governing rules, or style continually failed him. Finally, a critical incident occurred. Like many critical incidents in the transformational process, this one may seem comical to an outside observer.

On several occasions, the engineer's boss commented that he was very impressed with one of the engineer's subordinates. Finding the comment somewhat curious, the engineer finally asked for an explanation. The boss indicated that no matter how early he himself arrived at work, the subordinate's car was always there.

The engineer went to visit the subordinate and relayed that he had noticed that the subordinate always arrived at work before he did. The subordinate nodded his head and explained: "I have four teen-agers who wake up at dawn. The mornings at my house are chaotic. So I come in early. I read for awhile, then I write in my personal journal, read the paper, have some coffee, and then I start work at eight."

When the engineer left his subordinate's office, he was at first furious. But after a couple of minutes, he sat down and started to laugh. He later told me, "That is when I discovered perception." He went on to say that from that moment everything started to change. He became more patient. He began to experiment with participative decision making. His relationships with superiors gradually improved. Eventually he actually came to appreciate the need to think and operate in more complex ways at the higher levels of the organization.

This story follows the transformational cycle described in Chapter Two. The engineer's last promotion put him into the uncertainty phase. Here he applied his old assumptions and governing rules only to see them fail. This produced feelings of frustration and panic that in turn led him to try even harder. Not surprisingly, this resulted in more failure and frustration. Fortunately for him, he did not simply give up and resign from the company. Eventually there was enough frustration to weaken his existing paradigm, and an event occurred that gave him the critical, creative insight that he needed. This led him to reframe what it meant to manage. The human and political domains became integrated into his world view. This was followed by a marked improvement in performance.

A second illustration of a spontaneous change in style is found in a self-report written by David K. Hurst (1984). Hurst was the executive vice-president of Russell Steel, which is a subsidiary of Federal Industries, Ltd., of Canada. In 1979 Hurst was with Hugh Russell Inc., the fiftieth largest public company in his country. It was a very conventional company with three volumes of corporate policy spelling out a detailed, nuts-and-bolts approach to management.

In 1980 the company was acquired in a 100 percent leveraged buyout and became part of a very large and unprofitable steel fabricator, York Steel Construction. The resulting company was known as York Russell. On the eve of one of Canada's worst recessions, the new entity had $10 million in equity and $275 million in debt. What followed was a string of nightmarish crises. During this period, the company's objective shifted from growth to survival, its structure changed from a centralized to a decentralized one, and its focus shifted from making a profit to increasing cash flow. In the meantime, bankers and suppliers "swarmed" all over the company.

In the heat of the crisis everything that Hurst believed about "good management" melted away. In the midst of uncertainty a new paradigm emerged that even now, he is not sure he fully understands. The old "hard" framework (equivalent to the bottom half of the competing values framework) he calls the "box" approach, the new one (equivalent to the top half of the competing values framework) the "bubble" approach. The company shifted its emphasis from tasks to roles, from structures to groups, from information processes to networks, and from compensation systems to rewards. Boxes represent "hard" thought processes, while bubbles represent "soft" ones. When it was a question of arguing from the "box" perspectives, facts seemed very tangible and compelling. But from the bubble perspective, facts simply became abstractions based on a logical framework.

To cope with the financial crisis, it was necessary to set up numerous task forces. Information that had been closely guarded now had to be revealed. In the crisis, the task forces or teams, contrary to expectation, attacked their projects "with a passion." The groups were characterized by a warmth and trust that had not been present in the company before the crisis. The previous emphasis on decisiveness and hierarchical authority was suspended in favor of a new approach:

> Now we worry a good deal less about making decisions; they arise as fairly obvious conclusions

drawn from a mass of shared assumptions. It's
the assumptions that we spend our time working
on. One of our "producers" (an executive vice-
president) calls it "conditioning," and indeed it is.
Of course, making decisions this way requires that
senior management build networks with people
many layers down in the organization. This kind
of communication is directly at odds with the
communication policy laid down in the premerger
corporation, which emphasized direct-line reporting. . . . A consequence of this network information process is that we often have to wait for the
right time to make a decision. We call the wait a
"creative stall." In the old organization it would have
been called procrastination, but what we're doing
is waiting for some important layers to come "on-
side" before making an announcement. You "prepare in the box and wait in the bubble" [Hurst,
1984, p. 82].

Now that the crisis is over, the company finds both frameworks critical. Each is insufficient when used alone. And now
that the company is in a more stable condition, it consciously
works to use the strength of both frameworks. It deliberately
creates crises by choosing to reach out beyond an existing strategy or structure. It tries to infuse activities with symbolic importance, and it regularly engages in trust- and team-building
activities.

In considering the simultaneous presence of the two
schemes, Hurst indicates that his company now sees management as the task of balancing the polarities that are the essence
of organizational life. A successful organization must have a
bubble in every box and a box in every bubble. In describing the
outcomes of balancing polarities, Hurst writes, "The amazing
thing is that the process works so well. The spirit of cooperation
among senior managers is intense, and we seem to be getting
luckier as we go along. When a magic event takes place, it means
that somehow we got the timing just right. And there is great joy

in that" (p. 88). This statement is strikingly similar to that of Bill Russell in Chapter Two.

As with our engineer, Hurst and his colleagues were suddenly confronted with a highly uncertain situation in which their traditional approach was not working. Out of necessity, they developed a new model. It came not intellectually but through experience, that is, it evolved in a somewhat spontaneous manner. The new framework allowed them to greatly expand their approaches to problem solving. Of particular note is the fact that the new model did not preclude use of the old one. They were able to call upon either. Because the transformation occurred collectively, there was not only a discontinuous change in one person but a change in the culture of the entire system. Unlike the executives at J. C. Penney or PepsiCo, for example, Hurst and his colleagues were not blind to certain aspects of the competing values model. Instead they could simultaneously think in opposite ways.

Transformation Through Self-Examination

Not all transformations are the result of spontaneous processes. Torbert (1987) argues that they can also result from self-examination and the practice of action inquiry (see Chapter One). As an illustration he describes the case of Steve Thompson, a project manager for an underwater pipeline construction company. Torbert cites a self-study in which Thompson describes a critical incident between himself and his boss, Ron Cedrick.

The Setting. Ron Cedrick was a unique man. His appearance was not unlike George C. Scott's Patton. Minus the .45 caliber pistols, but wearing a shiny gold-colored metal hard hat, Ron Cedrick was aloof and distant. He was famous. He had single-handedly tamed the seven seas through engineering/construction feats. He worked for himself in constant demand from oil companies. He was to the offshore construction industry as Red

Adair was to oil-field fires. They traveled in the same circles, working for oil companies and commanding huge fees. The reason for this notoriety was simple. Ron Cedrick produced. No matter how difficult, the project always came in ahead of schedule.

British National Oil Company (BNOC) had contracted with him to manage the construction and installation of their "single anchor leg mooring (SALM) system." This system removed the need for flowing oil through hundreds of miles of pipeline from the offshore oil field to shore. Instead, this system enabled BNOC to fill oil tankers at sea in the oil field. The initial underwater construction had been completed in a deep, protected Norwegian fjord that was surrounded by majestic snow-capped mountains.

The calm of the picturesque fjord was behind us. It was February in the North Sea, gray, cold, wet, and rough. At that time of year, the North Sea could be unpredictably violent. We were onboard a 600-foot derrick ship, saturation diving to 540 feet below the surface of the North Sea. Saturation diving is a deep-sea diving procedure that enables two- to six-man diving teams to work at great depths without lost time for decompression. The divers, two per dive, work tethered from a diving submersible (bell) in a lightless, weightless, and hostile environment for periods of between eight and twelve hours per dive. Once the dive has been completed, the bell is winched back to the surface where it is mated to pressurized living chambers. The two divers then transfer under pressure from the bell to the dry living chambers on the deck of the ship. They remain pressurized until required to dive again.

The most critical part of this dangerous procedure is the launch and recovery of the bell through the interface. The interface is that area between the deck of the ship and twenty-five feet below the surface of the water—the wave-affected region. This is the area where the bell is most vulnerable to the surface condition of seas. Rough seas have separated more than one diving bell from its winch cable. When this happens, there is usually little hope of returning the divers alive.

The work had been challenging and different. The saturation divers and topside crew were doing an outstanding job. Ron Cedrick was extremely pleased with our performance. This was of particular importance to me because it was my first job as project manager.

My Behavior. The wind had changed directions and was coming at us from abeam, the same direction as the moderate swell. I did not like the looks of the sea. "It looks like it does before it really blows," I thought. The bell had just gone into the water for an anticipated twelve-hour run.

After alerting the shift supervisor to "keep an eye on the weather," I went up to the ship's bridge to have a look at the most recent weather forecast and facsimile. While I was reading the forecast that confirmed my suspicions, Ron Cedrick came up to me. "You and your boys have done a real fine job. I personally appreciate that and I know it will continue." He went on to explain that we had to complete the flowline connection today in order to be ahead of schedule. He said, "I know that the weather's gettin' up a bit, but those boys respect and will do what you ask—I've seen it. We need to keep that bell in the water just as long as we can before we let a little ole weather shut us down."

"Yes, sir," I responded confidently.

The outcome was all too predictable. I kept the bell in the water too long. The weather blew a gale. I pushed the diving operation beyond its safe limit. The recovery of the bell through twenty-foot seas was perilous. In the process, I not only compromised the safety of the divers but also set a poor precedent for the permissible operating parameters.

Feelings During the Event. I had an overwhelming desire to succeed. That desire was manifested by hard work, industriousness, and total task orientation. In defining or framing "success," I identified not only successful completion of the installation but also the satisfaction of Ron Cedrick as being synonymous with my success. After receiving positive reward from Ron Cedrick for the work we had completed in the fjord, I felt in conflict between my responsibilty to my fellow workers and fulfilling the expectation that Ron Cedrick had for our performance.

The moment I reviewed the weather forecast and facsimile, I became tense with fear. I was afraid that I would not have the strength of character to tell Ron Cedrick that I would have to shut down the operation. I was afraid that I would have to deceive the people who worked for me into thinking that pushing our safe operational limits was justified.

Finally, the awareness that I had manipulated my fellow workers and jeopardized the safety of the divers due to a weakness in my character destroyed my illusion that I was an honest, ethical man. I received none of the satisfaction from the reward given me by Ron Cedrick for "pulling it off"—we had completed the flowline connection [Torbert, 1987, pp. 162–164 (used by permission)].

According to Torbert, the writing exercise allowed Thompson to clearly identify an incongruity between his preferred self-image and his actual behavior. The heart of action inquiry is building integrity through the constant observation of one's lack of integrity.

Thompson's concerns were for the legitimacy of his overall operation and for his own self-respect. As he continued to write such self-studies, he became increasingly aware of his responsibility, not only for the technical aspects of his work but also for the "interpersonal, political, or ethical effects of his actions" (p. 165). He began to consciously develop new strategies.

Nine months after the self-examination process, Thompson's subordinates reported a dramatic change in him: "No longer merely a brittle, macho 'technical ace' who pushed himself and everyone else to the limit on particular jobs, he was now seen as a concerned, trustworthy, broad-visioned leader" (Torbert, 1987, p. 165). Three months later, he took a higher position, with a different firm, at double his salary. Three years later he was a company president.

According to Torbert, the most important lesson learned by Thompson was that there are a "galaxy of responses to any situation." Torbert goes on to argue:

> Paradoxically, then, the method by which the manager expands his or her sense of responsibility to include long-run issues of legitimacy and integrity, as well as short-run issues of efficiency and middle-run issues of effectiveness, is to pay more attention to the many influences operating at the immediate moment of decision. The very sense of being stuck between two uncomfortable alternatives — the proverbial "rock and a hard place" — comes to be taken as a sign to listen more carefully for other voices. The manager then molds an original solution that does justice to the complex of influences, both implementing and testing the solution through action inquiry.
>
> Most forms of professional knowledge result in conditional confidence — confidence that you will act well so long as the situation does not violate your assumptions about it. The active, awakening

attention described here results in unconditional confidence — confidence that you can meet any situation that arises because you are capable of discarding inaccurate assumptions and ineffective strategies in the midst of ongoing action [p. 168].

The notion of "unconditional confidence," described in Torbert's last sentence, is a hallmark of mastery in all areas of professional endeavor and particularly in the turbulent environment of higher-level management.

Possibility of Self-Improvement

There is a contrast between the last case and those of the engineer and the vice-president discussed earlier. The engineer and the vice-president "stumbled" into new paradigms. They discovered new frames because of certain spontaneous events. Steve Thompson's discovery came from a process of self-examination. He had deliberately undertaken an effort at self-improvement.

Conscious self-improvement is possible. Many managers, however, excuse themselves from this responsibility: "I am simply not creative, and there is no way to change that." "I hate details, and I will never be a good monitor." "Being a hard-driving producer is fine, but it is not worth the effort — life is simply too short." "Different people have different talents, and working with people is not my thing." In each case the statement is an excuse for not making changes. In each case the statement is untrue. It is always possible for someone to make improvements in his or her weak area. He or she may legitimately choose not to, since, as we learned in the last chapter, it is possible to somewhat neglect certain roles and still be effective. However, it is inaccurate to say, "It is not my style, I am not able." Although painful, it is in fact possible to make improvements in one's weak areas. Here I will outline a procedure for doing so.

Agenda for Self-Improvement

This agenda involves three general steps: Learn about yourself, develop a change strategy, and implement the strategy.

Exhibit 1. An Agenda for Self-Improvement.

---

1. Learn About Yourself
   ____ Complete the competing values instrument (See Chapter Nine)
   ____ Do a written self-evaluation of each role
   ____ Have others evaluate you with the instrument
   ____ Discuss the differences with people who will be honest
2. Develop a Change Strategy
   ____ Keep a journal
   ____ Identify specific areas in need of improvement
   ____ Identify role models for your weak areas
   ____ Read appropriate books (See Resource A)
3. Implement the Change Strategy
   ____ Be honest about the costs of improvement
   ____ Develop a social support system
   ____ Review the transformational cycle (Chapter Two)
   ____ Constantly evaluate and modify your strategy

Within these three steps are many key subpoints (see Exhibit 1). We have used this process with many managers and graduate students. In the beginning of the process, many participants are cynical, and some make only halfhearted efforts. Needless to say, they show little achievement. But others attack the process with zeal, and they naturally achieve considerably more. The interesting thing is that the people who make progress do so in whatever quadrant they choose. It is possible to learn in any area.

Learn About Yourself. The first step here is to do a self-assessment. This involves filling out the competing values instrument, analyzing your skills in each role, and doing a written assessment of yourself in each role. In the written assessment, you should explain why you believe you are strong or weak in each area.

   This step is a relatively painless but often misleading one. The majority of managers assess themselves in a more positive way than do their subordinates, peers, and superiors. This leads to a more difficult and painful step—obtaining honest feedback from others. It involves having others fill out the competing values instrument, and comparing the profile revealed by their data with your self-generated profile.

   While most of us claim that we want to receive honest feedback from those around us, we in fact behave in ways that prevent such feedback. In my M.B.A. classes I assign students to not only improve themselves in the course of a semester but to also go out and improve a manager. They arrange to act as consultants to a practicing manager; over the semester they analyze the manager's behavior and work with the person to improve weak areas. This provides an important mirror that allows the student to see the flaws and the resistances in themselves by seeing them first in another person. The following is a typical statement about feedback, written by one of my students:

"Perhaps one of the most amazing things to me is that, not only the manager we worked with, but virtually every manager that was helped by one of the teams in the class, was so deeply interested in feedback from subordinates and others. They were simply unsure what others thought about them. In every case, it was the first time in their careers that they received such feedback. As I think about it now, it seems incredible that such a simple thing could be so powerful."

Feedback from others is indeed powerful. Sometimes it can be too powerful. Occasionally a manager receives feedback suggesting that other people see him or her as less effective in a given area than the person sees him- or herself. While most managers can handle this negative message, some cannot, and this can be a cause of crisis. Some managers get depressed and withdraw, others get angry and want to punish those who gave the feedback. Neither response of course is healthy.

When you get feedback that comes as a surprise, I suggest that you use it as a base for honest exploration and discussion. First, wait long enough to get in the proper frame of mind that you are indeed ready to hear what people have to say. This may take some time and preparation. Go to those people who know you best, ask questions about the data that you have received, and then "listen" to what they have to say. This strategy takes maturity and self-esteem. If you feel unsure of yourself, you should wait until some future time to seek feedback. Be careful not to behave in ways that force people to say what you want to hear.

You may feel unable, for whatever reason, to approach particular people for feedback, but that should not be a cause for concern. In fact, it is a common occurrence. People should talk to those few others with whom they have a trusting relationship but who will nevertheless be honest in their feedback.

Develop a Change Strategy. A key element in developing such a strategy is to keep a journal. In this journal you should record the self-analysis outlined above. You should then employ the journal as you engage in the steps described below.

Once all the data, both quantitative and qualitative, have been gathered, you might then make a final assessment of what you think your strong and weak areas are. As you write a final assessment of your strengths and weaknesses in each role of the competing values framework, pinpoint the ones you most need to work on. In doing so you should also identify someone who does very well in your weak role. This will help to make concrete the kinds of behaviors that are appropriate in this role. When you are in situations that call for behavior in the role, you can ask yourself, What would the person do in this situation?

This step sometimes makes people uncomfortable because they may not like the people who do well in their weak areas. For example, I have a colleague who, in terms of the competing values framework, is my exact opposite in outlook, strategy, and behavior. My weak roles are his strongest. Working with him is very difficult. We have conflict over nearly every decision that we are mutually involved in. I see many of his assumptions as being almost immoral. Interestingly, although I cannot comprehend why, he sees many of my assumptions in a similar way.

While the costs of working with him have been high, I have also learned a great deal from him. In many situations I have watched him do the exact opposite of what I would have done. It sometimes has been shocking to see his strategies work far better than my own. Over time I have come to recognize certain situations in which his thinking might be better than mine. I am now able to stop before implementing my natural strategy and ask myself what he would do in this case. Often I am dissatisfied with the answer and proceed with my own approach. There are, however, times when I go against my instincts and follow his lead. Thinking about him as a role model in my weak areas enlarges my pool of possible strategies. Sometimes, following uncomfortable strategies results in the development of a wider array of behaviors and skills.

Another key activity is to read literature that is related to your weak roles. In Resource A you will find a copy of the competing values reading list. It is organized according to the eight roles in the competing values framework. There are approximately fifteen to twenty books listed under each role. Some are self-improvement books, others are professional management books. Most are very basic. Many managers have used the list as a source of ideas on how to better play a particular role.

I suggest that you select the most relevant books and read them very rapidly. Then briefly record any useful ideas in your notebook. On a regular basis, consolidate these ideas into action strategies that you would like to try.

Implement the Strategy. After you finish analyzing your strengths and weaknesses, considering role models, reading for ideas, and consolidating insights into possible action strategies, it is time to experiment. The first step in the experimental process is to be honest about the costs of improvement. Many people simply are not interested in changing, while others are so idealistic and impatient that they quickly become disillusioned by the failures that they encounter. The improvement process involves some exertion.

Because it is not always easy to engage in this process, I suggest developing a social support system. The key is to find someone to talk to. In executive development seminars I conduct, many managers choose their immediate superiors to play this role. When appropriate, this can be a very significant and effective arrangement. But others feel uncomfortable with their superiors and select some other person at work. Still others choose a spouse. Whoever is selected, arrange a schedule that will allow you to regularly meet with that person to discuss your failures and successes. This person will often be able to provide encouragement and creative insights.

As you begin to experiment with new strategies and behaviors, keep in mind the transformational cycle discussed in Chapter Two. Getting off a plateau usually involves some risk. It sometimes means moving into a situation that requires assumptions very different from those with which you are familiar. Instead of trying to avoid failure, you may need to embrace failure and to see it as an indispensable part of the learning process.

As you engage in your intuitive experiments, constantly evaluate your progress. Keep your notebook close at hand. Record and analyze failures, record insights, modify your strategies. Follow the example of Steve Thompson earlier in the chapter. You will be impressed with the power of constant self-evaluation. One manager scored low on the broker role and was very concerned about his inability to make persuasive presentations. He worked through all the above steps and reported a dramatic improvement in performance. Here is what he wrote about the process of self-evaluation:

> I had never before kept a journal. It was very hard for me to get used to the idea. But I was intense about trying to improve, and it was clear that a journal was going to be important. I read everything I could get my hands on and I made lots of notes. Whenever anyone made a presentation of any kind, a salesman, a politician, a young kid in my Sunday school class, I would analyze what was effective and what was not. Each time I drew lessons for myself. Whenever I made a presentation, I would immediately find some time to do a self-analysis. I was a tough self-critic.
>
> Every so often, I would make notes of my notes. That is, I would reduce them to a list of those principles that seemed to be most important for me. I was, without knowing it, building my own personal theory of persuasive speaking. The important thing is that it was an applied theory. It told me "how to." After four months or so, I really started to

show signs of progress. People told me they were amazed at how much better I was doing.

The improvement process is sometimes easier than one thinks it is going to be. One manager took an M.B.A. class in which we used this material. His competing values profile suggested that he was very strong in all the roles except that of monitor. He saw himself as a visionary, and he thought that being a monitor was simply "not his style." Hence, it was with some dread that he undertook the implementation of the steps outlined earlier. Here is his report:

"I picked a role model, read some books, made some notes, and designed a change program. It was really very simple. Basically it boiled down to setting times to do a whole raft of tasks that I normally ignore. That is all there was to it. I was amazed. It was not a matter of ability, it was actually quite easy. It is now hard to believe that I once thought that I was incapable of doing the things in the monitor role."

In summary, it is possible to become a better manager, particularly to improve in those areas that seem far from your natural style. Here I have outlined a few simple steps. When applied in a serious way, they can be very helpful in moving you forward along the road to mastery.

9

Assessment and Skill-Building Exercises

This chapter provides a number of instruments that may be of use in the process of self-assessment and self-improvement. The first section contains an instrument for assessing present behavior, and section two has a workbook for writing out a preliminary self-assessment and change process. Section three provides two instruments: the first gives a profile of perceived organizational performance and the second, developed by Kim S. Cameron, makes possible a multilevel analysis of organizational culture.

For further information, the reader is referred to the three resources at the back of this volume. Resource A is a reading list organized according to the competing values framework. It can be used to locate information in a desired area. Resource B contains the extended version of the competing values leadership instrument. And Resource C presents a list of interview questions based on the competing values approach.

Self-Knowledge: Assessing Managerial Behaviors

This section contains two copies of an instrument that can be used to assess various managerial behaviors. You can use the first version of the instrument to assess yourself, and you can copy the second version and distribute it to subordinates, peers, and superiors. Because the second version of the instrument provides standardized scores, based on the sample of managers in Chapter Seven, you can compare the results with the profiles of effective and ineffective managers in that chapter.

Exhibit 2. Competing Values Leadership Instrument: Self-Assessment.

Listed below are some statements that describe management behaviors. You should indicate how often you engage in these behaviors. Please use the following scale to respond to each statement. Place a number from 1 to 7 in the space just before each of the items.

Very infrequently   1   2   3   4   5   6   7   Very frequently

---

In doing my job, I
_____   1. listen to the personal problems of subordinates.
_____   2. meticulously review detailed reports.
_____   3. influence decisions made at higher levels.
_____   4. do problem solving in creative, clever ways.
_____   5. clearly define areas of responsibility for subordinates.
_____   6. display a wholehearted commitment to the job.
_____   7. facilitate consensus building in work-group sessions.
_____   8. protect continuity in day-to-day operations.
_____   9. compare records, reports, and so on to detect any discrepancies in them.
_____ 10. show empathy and concern in dealing with subordinates.
_____ 11. set clear objectives for the work unit.
_____ 12. search for innovations and potential improvements.
_____ 13. work on maintaining a network of influential contacts.
_____ 14. insist on minimum disruption to the work flow.
_____ 15. reflect high motivation for my role.
_____ 16 encourage participative decision making in work-group sessions.

In a multimethod-multitrait analysis of the data in Chapter Seven, Quinn, Faerman, and Dixit (1987) have found that the instrument has both convergent and discriminant validity. Reliability scores are also high. The scales, however, are limited to two items per scale, and researchers may want to employ the more fully developed instruments in Resource B.

Self-Assessment: Computing Your Scores. What follows is a worksheet that will allow you to compute your scores. Completing the worksheet is fairly simple:

1. Record all the scores from the self-assessment exercise. For example, suppose on items number 7 and number 16, you gave yourself scores of 5 and 6. On the lines under facilitator, you would write a 5 and a 6 next to number 7 and number 16. Do this for all sixteen items.

Exhibit 3. Computational Worksheet for Self-Assessment.

The Facilitator		The Mentor	
#7	____	#1	____
#16	____	#10	____
Total	____	Total	____
The Innovator		The Broker	
#4	____	#3	____
#12	____	#13	____
Total	____	Total	____
The Producer		The Director	
#6	____	#5	____
#15	____	#11	____
Total	____	Total	____
The Coordinator		The Monitor	
#8	____	#2	____
#14	____	#9	____
Total	____	Total	____

2. Total the two scores under each role. In the illustration given above, you would add 5 plus 6 to get a total of 11. Compute the total for all eight roles.

3. Divide each total by 2. Continuing with the same illustration, you would simply divide 11 by 2, obtaining a result of 5.5. Put 5.5 on the blank line after the word *Total.* Follow the same procedure for all eight roles.

Self-Assessment: Drawing Your Profile. Drawing your own profile is also a fairly simple process. It merely involves transferring your scores from the worksheet to Figure 18 and then connecting the scores by drawing lines between them.

First, locate your final score for a given role. Following the example from the last set of instructions, let us assume that it is 5.5 for the facilitator role. Go to the facilitator role on the diagram. Find the point marked with the number 5. Each dot equals .20, so you would make a mark halfway between the second and third dots.

Repeat the above process for each of the remaining scores. When you are finished, there should be a small mark representing a score on each of the eight roles.

Figure 18. Self-Assessment: Your Own Profile.

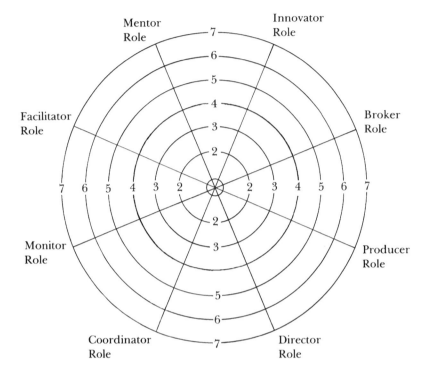

To complete your profile, draw as straight a line as possible between each of the eight scores. You should then have a complete profile.

The View of Others: Computing the Scores

Following are a questionnaire and worksheet for computing the scores on the preceding exercise. The numbers and formulas on the computational worksheet allow you to compute standard scores and compare your results to the scores of the managers studied in Chapter Seven. In other words, you will obtain a standardized profile that is comparable to the profiles in Chapter Seven. The process is fairly simple:

    1. Record all the scores from the questionnaire. For ex-

Exhibit 4. Competing Values Leadership Instrument: The View of Others.

Listed below are some statements that describe management behaviors. You should indicate how often the person you are describing engages in these behaviors. Please use the following scale to respond to each statement. Place a number from 1 to 7 in the space just before each of the items.

Very infrequently   1   2   3   4   5   6   7   Very frequently

In doing the job, this person
____ 1. listens to the personal problems of subordinates.
____ 2. meticulously reviews detailed reports.
____ 3. influences decisions made at higher levels.
____ 4. does problem solving in creative, clever ways.
____ 5. clearly defines areas of responsibility for subordinates.
____ 6. displays a wholehearted commitment to the job.
____ 7. facilitates consensus building in work-group sessions.
____ 8. protects continuity in day-to-day operations.
____ 9. compares records, reports, and so on to detect any discrepancies in them.
____ 10. shows empathy and concern in dealing with subordinates.
____ 11. sets clear objectives for the work unit.
____ 12. searches for innovations and potential improvements.
____ 13. works on maintaining a network of influential contacts.
____ 14. insists on minimum disruption to the work flow.
____ 15. reflects high motivation for the role.
____ 16 encourages participative decision making in work-group sessions.

ample, suppose on items number 7 and number 16, the respondent gave you scores of 5 and 6. On the lines under facilitator, you would write a 5 and a 6 next to number 7 and number 16. Do this for all sixteen items.

2. Total the two scores under each role. Continuing with the same illustration, you would add 5 plus 6 to get a total of 11. Compute the total for all eight roles.

3. Divide each total by 2. In the illustration used above, you would simply divide 11 by 2, obtaining a result of 5.5. Put 5.5 on the blank line after the first parenthesis. Do this for all eight roles.

4. Subtract from the above result the number indicated. Continuing the example, subtract 4.1 from 5.5 to obtain a result of 1.4. Do this for all eight roles.

Exhibit 5. Computational Worksheet for Your Assessment by Others.

The Facilitator	The Mentor
#7 ___	#1 ___
#16 ___	#10 ___
Total ___ ÷ 2 = (___ − 4.1) ÷ 1.2 = ___	Total ___ ÷ 2 = (___ − 4.6) ÷ 1.5 = ___
The Innovator	The Broker
#4 ___	#3 ___
#12 ___	#13 ___
Total ___ ÷ 2 = (___ − 4.3) ÷ 1.1 = ___	Total ___ ÷ 2 = (___ − 4.6) ÷ 1.4 = ___
The Producer	The Director
#6 ___	#5 ___
#15 ___	#11 ___
Total ___ ÷ 2 = (___ − 5.1) ÷ 1.2 = ___	Total ___ ÷ 2 = (___ − 4.2) ÷ 1.1 = ___
The Coordinator	The Monitor
#8 ___	#2 ___
#14 ___	#9 ___
Total ___ ÷ 2 = (___ − 3.9) ÷ 1.0 = ___	Total ___ ÷ 2 = (___ − 4.0) ÷ 1.0 = ___

5. Divide the above result by the number indicated. Continuing the example, divide 1.4 by 1.2. The result is 1.166, which rounds off to 1.17. This is your standard score on the facilitator role. Do this for all eight roles.

6. For each instrument filled out by another person, repeat the same procedure. Then add the scores for each role and compute an average standard score. For example, if four people gave you scores on the facilitator role of 1.18, 1.25, .95, and 1.14, you would add these, getting a total of 4.52. You would then compute an average by dividing by 4. Thus, your score on the facilitator role would be 1.13.

Drawing Your Profile as Others View It. Drawing your own profile as others view you merely involves transferring your scores from the worksheet to Figure 19 and then connecting the scores by drawing lines between them.

First, locate your final score for a given role. Following the example from the last set of instructions, let us assume that it is 1.13 for the facilitator role. Go to the facilitator role on the diagram. Your score in this case is greater than zero, that is, it is a positive rather than a negative number. (Remember zero is the mean or 50th percentile.) Move up to the line marked with num-

Figure 19. Your Profile as Others View It.

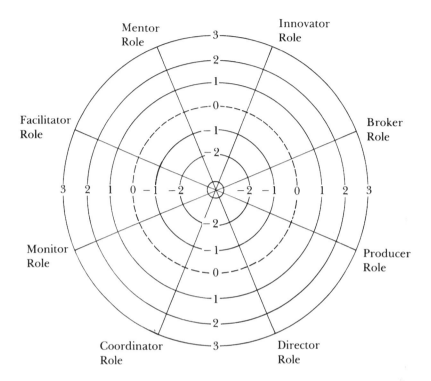

ber 1. Now go up to .13 above the line. Each dot equals .20, so you make a mark just below the first dot, above the line marked 1.

Repeat this process for each of the remaining scores. When you are finished, there should be a small mark representing a score on each of the eight roles.

To complete your profile, draw as straight a line as possible between each of the eight scores. You should then have a complete profile of your managerial abilities as viewed by others.

Self-Assessment and Change: A Competing Values Workbook

This section contains a workbook that describes each of the eight roles in the competing values framework. It then asks three sets of questions about each role. The workbook is meant as a tool for thinking in greater depth about yourself and what you might do to improve your managerial abilities.

The Producer

A producer is expected to be task-oriented and work focused and to have high interest, motivation, energy, and personal drive. In this role a manager is supposed to encourage subordinates to accept responsibility, complete assignments, and maintain high productivity. This usually involves stimulating unit members to better accomplish stated goals.

1. *Learn About Yourself*
   In regard to this role, what do I know about myself? What do others think of my performance in this role and why?
2. *Develop a Change Strategy*
   How could I more effectively play this role? Who are some people I could imitate? What books should I read?
3. *Implement the Change Strategy*
   What specific objectives and deadlines should I set? With whom should I share these? How will I evaluate my performance?

The Director

As a director, a manager is expected to clarify expectations through processes such as planning and goal setting and to be a decisive initiator who defines problems, selects alternatives, establishes objectives, defines roles and tasks, generates rules and policies, evaluates performance, and gives instructions.

1. *Learn About Yourself*
   In regard to this role, what do I know about myself? What do others think of my performance in this role and why?

2. *Develop a Change Strategy*
    How could I more effectively play this role? Who are some people I could imitate? What books should I read?
3. *Implement the Change Strategy*
    What specific objectives and deadlines should I set? With whom should I share these? How will I evaluate my performance?

The Broker

The broker is particularly concerned with maintaining external legitimacy and obtaining resources. In carrying out this role, the manager is expected to be politically astute, persuasive, influential, and powerful. Image, appearance, and reputation are important. As a broker, the manager is expected to meet with people from outside the unit, to represent, negotiate, market, act as a liaison and spokesperson, and to acquire resources.

1. *Learn About Yourself*
    In regard to this role, what do I know about myself? What do others think of my performance in this role and why?
2. *Develop a Change Strategy*
    How could I more effectively play this role? Who are some people I could imitate? What books should I read?
3. *Implement the Change Strategy*
    What specific objectives and deadlines should I set? With whom should I share these? How will I evaluate my performance?

The Innovator

As an innovator, a manager is expected to facilitate adaptation and change. The innovator conceptualizes and projects needed changes. Unlike the monitor role, where deduction, facts, and quantitative analysis rule, the innovator role requires the manager to be a creative dreamer who sees the future, envisions innovations, and packages them in inviting ways.

1. *Learn About Yourself*
   In regard to this role, what do I know about myself? What do others think of my performance in this role and why?
2. *Develop a Change Strategy*
   How could I more effectively play this role? Who are some people I could imitate? What books should I read?
3. *Implement the Change Strategy*
   What specific objectives and deadlines should I set? With whom should I share these? How will I evaluate my performance?

The Facilitator

The facilitator is expected to foster collective effort, to build cohesion and teamwork, and to manage interpersonal conflict. In this role the leader is described as process oriented. Expected behaviors include mediating interpersonal disputes, using conflict reduction techniques, developing cohesion and morale, obtaining input and participation, and facilitating group problem solving.

1. *Learn About Yourself*
   In regard to this role, what do I know about myself? What do others think of my performance in this role and why?
2. *Develop a Change Strategy*
   How could I more effectively play this role? Who are some people I could imitate? What books should I read?
3. *Implement the Change Strategy*
   What specific objectives and deadlines should I set? With whom should I share these? How will I evaluate my performance?

The Mentor

The mentor is expected to engage in the development of people through a caring, empathetic orientation. In this role the leader is expected to be helpful, considerate, sensitive, approachable, open, and fair. In acting out this role, the manager listens, supports legitimate requests, conveys appreciation, and gives compliments and credit. He or she sees people as resources to be developed. The leader helps with skill building, provides training opportunities, and helps people develop plans for their own individual development.

1. *Learn About Yourself*
   In regard to this role, what do I know about myself? What do others think of my performance in this role and why?
2. *Develop a Change Strategy*
   How could I more effectively play this role? Who are some people I could imitate? What books should I read?
3. *Implement the Change Strategy*
   What specific objectives and deadlines should I set? With whom should I share these? How will I evaluate my performance?

The Monitor

As a monitor, a manager is expected to know what is going on in the unit, to determine whether people are complying with the rules, and to see if the unit is meeting its quotas. The monitor must have a passion for details and be good at rational analysis. Behaviors in this role include technical analysis, dealing with routine information, and logical problem solving.

1. *Learn About Yourself*
   In regard to this role, what do I know about myself? What do others think of my performance in this role and why?
2. *Develop a Change Strategy*
   How could I more effectively play this role? Who are some people I could imitate? What books should I read?
3. *Implement the Change Strategy*
   What specific objectives and deadlines should I set? With whom should I share these? How will I evaluate my performance?

The Coordinator

As a coordinator, a manager is expected to maintain the structure and flow of the system. The person in this role is expected to be dependable and reliable. Behaviors include protecting continuity, minimizing disruptions, doing paper work, reviewing and evaluating reports, writing budgets, and writing and coordinating plans and proposals.

1. *Learn About Yourself*
   In regard to this role, what do I know about myself? What do others think of my performance in this role and why?
2. *Develop a Change Strategy*
   How could I more effectively play this role? Who are some people I could imitate? What books should I read?
3. *Implement the Change Strategy*
   What specific objectives and deadlines should I set? With whom should I share these? How will I evaluate my performance?

An Overall Strategy

1. *Learning*
   Given the analyses on the previous pages, what are my most significant overall learnings? What are my most important strengths and weaknesses?
2. *Change Strategies*
   Overall, what are the most important things I will do differently? What are the most important changes I need to make?
3. *Implement the Change Strategy*
   What are my most important overall objectives? How will I implement and evaluate them?

Organizational Knowledge: Assessing Performance and Culture

This section includes two different instruments. The first instrument measures perceptions of organizational perfor-

Exhibit 6. Competing Values Organizational Effectiveness Instrument.

Listed below are some statements that describe organizational performance. You should indicate how often they occur in your unit. Please use the following scale to respond to each statement. Place a number from 1 to 7 in the space just before each of the items.

Very infrequently   1   2   3   4   5   6   7   Very frequently

____ 1. The work process is coordinated and under control.
____ 2. Participative decision making is widely and appropriately employed.
____ 3. Rules, procedures, and formal methods guide the work.
____ 4. The goals are clearly understood by most members.
____ 5. The work effort is usually intense.
____ 6. There is a stable, predictable work environment.
____ 7. Innovation is stressed.
____ 8. There is a positive interpersonal climate.
____ 9. Quantification and measurement are key parts of the work climate.
____ 10. Consensual decision making is encouraged.
____ 11. Outsiders perceive it as a vibrant, high-potential unit.
____ 12. Creative insights, hunches, and innovative ideas are encouraged.
____ 13. It is easy to give an explanation of the overall objectives of the unit.
____ 14. There is a constant striving for greater accomplishment.
____ 15. Employees feel as though they really belong to the unit.
____ 16. The unit has the image of a growing, dynamic system.

mance. The second instrument provides a multilevel view of organizational culture.

First Instrument. This can be used to generate a standardized profile consistent with those presented in earlier chapters. The instrument has been developed to reflect the competing values framework in its most recent form. Standardized scores are based on the responses of 206 managers who described their work units. The sample, described in Chapter Seven, represents a wide array of organizational units in all parts of the country. Data analysis suggests that there is discriminant validity, and reliability scores are high. The interrelationship between scales follows the competing values framework. The scales are, however, based on only two items each. Research is underway to increase the number of items in the scales. An earlier and more lengthy instrument is also available (Rohrbaugh, 1981).

Organizational Effectiveness: Computing Your Scores. The worksheet that follows will allow you to compute your scores on the effectiveness instrument. The numbers and formulas on the computational worksheet will allow you to compare your own scores on the instrument with a diverse sample of organizational units. The process is fairly simple:

1. Record all the scores from the effectiveness instrument. For example, suppose that on items number 2 and number 10 you gave yourself scores of 5 and 6. On the lines under participation, next to number 2 and number 10, you would write a 5 and a 6. Do this for all sixteen items.

2. Total the two scores under each area. In the illustration given above, you would add 5 plus 6 to get a total of 11. Compute the total for all eight areas.

3. Divide each total by 2. In the illustration, you would simply divide 11 by 2, obtaining a result of 5.5. Put 5.5 on the blank line after the first parenthesis. Do this for all eight areas.

Exhibit 7. Computational Worksheet for Organizational Effectiveness.

Participation, Openness	*Commitment, Morale*
#2 ___	#8 ___
#10 ___	#15 ___
Total ___ $\div$ 2 = (___ − 3.6) $\div$ 1.2 = ___	Total ___ $\div$ 2 = (___ − 4.2) $\div$ 1.1 = ___
Innovation, Adaptation	*External Support, Growth*
#7 ___	#11 ___
#12 ___	#16 ___
Total ___ $\div$ 2 = (___ − 4.0) $\div$ 1.1 = ___	Total ___ $\div$ 2 = (___ − 4.5) $\div$ 1.3 = ___
Productivity, Accomplishment	*Direction, Goal Clarity*
#5 ___	#4 ___
#14 ___	#13 ___
Total ___ $\div$ 2 = (___ − 4.6) $\div$ 1.1 = ___	Total ___ $\div$ 2 = (___ − 4.4) $\div$ 1.1 = ___
Stability, Control	*Documentation, Information Management*
#1 ___	#3 ___
#6 ___	#9 ___
Total ___ $\div$ 2 = (___ − 4.1) $\div$ 1.0 = ___	Total ___ $\div$ 2 = (___ − 4.5) $\div$ 1.2 = ___

Figure 20. Organizational Effectiveness: Drawing Your Profile.

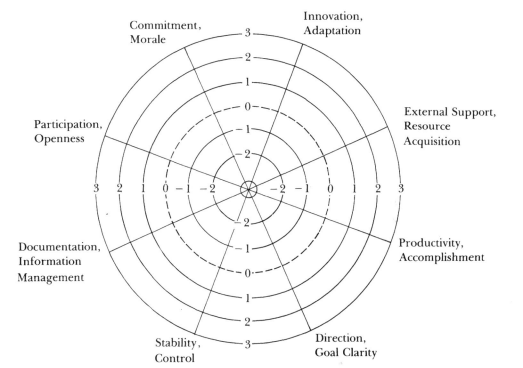

4. Subtract from the above result the number indicated. Continuing the example, subtract 3.6 from 5.5 to obtain a result of 1.9. Do this for all eight areas.

5. Divide the above result by the number indicated. Continuing the example, divide 1.9 by 1.2. The result is 1.583. This is your standard score for productivity. Follow the same procedure for all eight areas.

Organizational Effectiveness: Drawing Your Profile. Drawing your own profile for organizational effectiveness is a fairly simple process. It merely involves transferring your scores from the worksheet to Figure 20 and then connecting the scores by drawing lines between them.

First, locate your final score for a given role. Following the

Exhibit 8. Diagnosing Corporate Culture.

Please answer the following six questions on corporate culture. You can use the data from these items to diagnose your own corporate culture and to compare it to the perceptions of others.

Each of these items contains four descriptions of organizations. Please distribute 100 points among the four descriptions depending on how similar the description is to your own organization. None of the descriptions is any better than the others; they are just different. For each question, please use 100 points.

In question 1, for example, if organization A seems very similar to mine, B seems somewhat similar, and C and D do not seem similar at all, I might give 70 points to A and the remaining 30 points to B.

1. Dominant Characteristics (Divide 100 points.)
   a. _____ Organization A is a very personal place. It is like an extended family. People seem to share a lot of themselves.
   b. _____ Organization B is a very dynamic and entrepreneurial place. People are willing to stick their necks out and take risks.
   c. _____ Organization C is a very formalized and structured place. Bureaucratic procedures generally govern what people do.
   d. _____ Organization D is very competitive in orientation. A major concern is with getting the job done. People are very production and achievement oriented.

2. Organizational Leader (Divide 100 points.)
   a. _____ The head of organization A is generally considered to be a mentor, a facilitator, or a parent figure.
   b. _____ The head of organization B is generally considered to be an entrepreneur, an innovator, or a risk taker.
   c. _____ The head of organization C is generally considered to be a coordinator, an organizer, or an efficiency expert.
   d. _____ The head of organization D is generally considered to be a hard driver, a producer, or a competitor.

3. Organizational Glue (Divide 100 points.)
   a. _____ The glue that holds organization A together is loyalty and commitment. Cohesion and teamwork are characteristic of this organization.
   b. _____ The glue that holds organization B together is a focus on innovation and development. The emphasis is on being at the cutting edge.
   c. _____ The glue that holds organization C together is formal procedures, rules, or policies. Maintaining a smooth-running organization is important.
   d. _____ The glue that holds organization D together is an emphasis on production and goal accomplishment. Marketplace aggressiveness is a common theme.

4. Organizational Climate (Divide 100 points.)
   a. _____ The climate inside organization A is participative and comfortable. High trust and openness exist.

b. ____ The climate inside organization B emphasizes dynamism and readiness to meet new challenges. Trying new things and trial-and-error learning are common.

c. ____ The climate inside organization C emphasizes permanence and stability. Expectations regarding procedures are clear and enforced.

d. ____ The climate inside organization D is competitive and confrontational. Emphasis is placed on beating the competition.

5. Criteria of Success (Divide 100 points.)

a. ____ Organization A defines success on the basis of its development of human resources, teamwork, and concern for people.

b. ____ Organization B defines success on the basis of its having unique or the newest products. It is a product leader and innovator.

c. ____ Organization C defines success on the basis of efficiency. Dependable delivery, smooth scheduling, and low-cost production are critical.

d. ____ Organization D defines success on the basis of market penetration and market share. Being number one relative to the competition is a key objective.

6. Management Style (Divide 100 points.)

a. ____ The management style in organization A is characterized by teamwork, consensus, and participation.

b. ____ The management style in organization B is characterized by individual initiative, innovation, freedom, and uniqueness.

c. ____ The management style in organization C is characterized by security of employment, longevity in position, and predictability.

d. ____ The management style in organization D is characterized by hard-driving competitiveness, production, and achievement.

Source: Cameron, 1985. Reprinted by permission.

example from the last set of instructions, let us assume that it is 1.17 for the facilitator role. Go to the facilitator role on the diagram. Your score in this case is greater than zero, that is, it is a positive rather than a negative number. (Remember that zero is the mean or 50th percentile.) Move up to the line marked with the number 1. Now go up to .17 above the line. Each dot equals .20, so you make a mark just below the first dot, above the line marked 1.

Repeat this process for each of the remaining scores. When you are finished, there should be a small mark representing a score on each of the eight roles.

To complete your profile, draw as straight a line as possi-

Exhibit 9. Overall Profile for Organization Culture Type

In the spaces below, sum the points given to organization A (alternative *a*) for all eight items. Then divide by eight to obtain an average number of points for organization A. Do the same for the points you assigned to organizations B, C, and D.

Total Points Assigned		*Average Points for*
_____ Organization A items	divided by 6	_____ Organization A
_____ Organization B items	divided by 6	_____ Organization B
_____ Organization C items	divided by 6	_____ Organization C
_____ Organization D items	divided by 6	_____ Organization D

ble between each of the eight scores. You should then have a complete profile.

Second Instrument. This questionnaire was developed by Kim S. Cameron, now at the Department of Organizational Behavior, University of Michigan. The instrument yields six dimensions of organizational culture. These are plotted by transferring the scores from the six questions to the profile sheet containing six matrices. The scores from each of the questions can then be summed and averaged to obtain an overall cultural profile for the organization. The second profile sheet provides a summary matrix for this purpose.

This instrument has been administered in over 500 organizations, including colleges, banks, health care organizations, professional associations, and manufacturing firms. It has been used to assess departmental and divisional culture as well as overall organizational culture. It differs from most assessment instruments for organizational culture in providing respondents with descriptions of organizations. Respondents are then asked to identify the extent to which their organization is similar to the description. A common criticism of assessments of

Figure 21. Organizational Culture Plots.

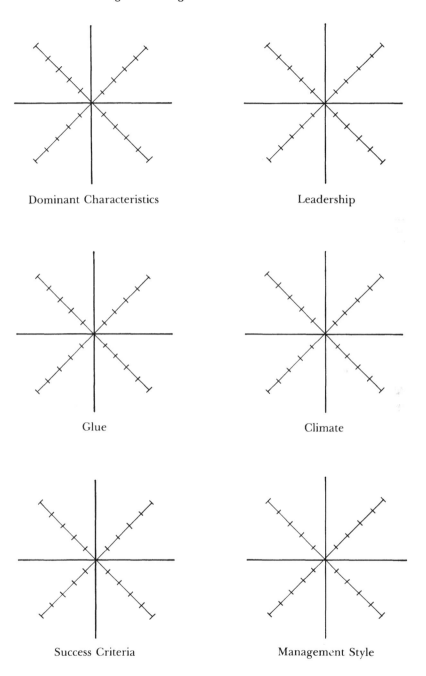

Dominant Characteristics   Leadership

Glue   Climate

Success Criteria   Management Style

Figure 22. Overall Culture Plot.

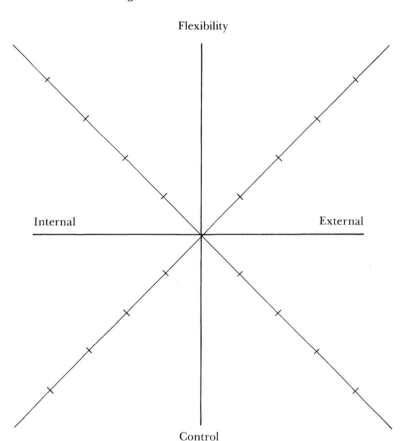

culture using questionnaires is that respondents' answers reflect only their personal attitudes. This produces organizational "climate" data, not cultural data. Underlying perspectives and values that characterize culture are not reflected in Likert-type questions. The advantage of this second instrument is that it serves as a mirror against which respondents can reflect the actual culture of their organizations. The underlying assumptions and values present in the organization are, therefore, more likely to emerge from the responses.

Past research using the questionnaire suggests that the instrument is internally reliable and is strongly associated with different types of organizational performance (see Cameron, 1985, for a study of the relationship between culture and effectiveness using this instrument). An important advantage of the instrument, however, is that the strength and congruence of organizational culture can be assessed as well as the type of culture present. One can measure how strongly an organization emphasizes a certain set of values or characteristics as well as the extent to which a variety of dimensions of the organization are congruent (for example, strategies, management style, and criteria of effectiveness). Contrary to common assumptions, research suggests that type of culture is more important than strength and congruence of culture in predicting organizational effectiveness (Cameron, 1985).

In plotting the results on the first profile sheet (Figure 21), keep in mind that alternative *a* in every question should be plotted in the upper-right-hand quadrant of each matrix. Alternative *b* should be plotted in the upper-right-hand quadrant. Alternative *c* is in the lower-left-hand quadrant, and alternative *d* is in the lower-right-hand quadrant. Each hash mark should be counted as 10 points. In some cases the plots may need to extend beyond the line (when, for example, 60 or 70 points are given to an alternative). Summing and averaging the *a* alternatives, the *b* alternatives, and so on for all six questions produces an overall cultural profile. It should be plotted on the overall profile sheet (Figure 22). Some kind of four-sided figure will result, often resembling a kite. This figure identifies the quadrants most emphasized by the culture of the organization.

10

Teaching Management Skills Using the Competing Values Model: A Case Study

There are at least two approaches to improving managerial performance. The first and most common involves the transfer of information. In this approach, it is assumed that facts and knowledge bring change. If a person needs to improve, he or she might be asked to read a book on management or attend a course or training session that would provide the necessary information. While this is a useful and important step, it is the equivalent of telling the little girl, from Chapter Two, who wants to ride a bicycle, that if she turns the handlebars and keeps pedaling, she will stay up, and then turning from her and walking away. It may be good information, but it is not likely to help her much. Most of the management courses in America do this very thing. Instructors give lectures on the theories of management (some useful and some not so useful) and assume that, if the information can be repeated back on an exam, the student knows how to manage. Because this assumption is so questionable, many institutions are increasingly turning their attention to a second approach.

The focus of this second approach is much less on information giving and much more on skill development. Here key skills are identified. As in the first approach, participants are

Note: Portions of this chapter are taken from an article by S. R. Faerman, R. E. Quinn, and M. P. Thompson (1987), entitled "Bridging Management Practice and Theory." Used by permission.

instructed in how to perform, but they are then asked to try the new behaviors by doing exercises in the classroom. They practice the new skills in the same way the little girl gets on the bicycle and tries to ride.

In this chapter I will review the history of a curriculum development and instructional project. The project was designed around the competing values framework and involved a number of problems, including the identification of skills and a method for skill development.

Project Background

Several years ago, I was involved in a systematic and global approach to skill building. This was undertaken in New York State. Two core curricula for a management education and development program were designed for practicing managers. The two curricula, one at the individual and the other at the organizational level, were built around the competing values framework. They were designed by an advisory committee of management education and development experts from across the United States. Curriculum development followed a skill-based approach to learning. These curricula are currently being delivered by management schools in fifteen different public and private colleges and universities in New York State. What follows is a description of the process used to select the specific skills included in each course, the process used to generate the two curricula, and the implementation and impact of the curricula after the first year of their implementation.

The Public Service Training Program is sponsored jointly by the New York State Governor's Office of Employee Relations and the New York State Public Employees Federation, an affiliate of the AFL-CIO, that represents New York State employees in the Professional, Scientific, and Technical (PS&T) bargaining unit. The program was originally funded for $3.5 million and is administered by the Nelson A. Rockefeller College of Public Affairs and Policy at the State University of New York at Albany, on behalf of higher education institutions in New York.

The program is designed to be taught at the graduate

level and consists of three components: public administration in New York State for PS&T employees, professional workshops, and course offerings. While the last two components involve the development and delivery of courses in a wide range of professional fields and specialized areas, the first component focuses on the development and delivery of two core management curricula. The first curriculum, entitled Program in Supervision, is intended for new managers; the second, entitled Program in Administration curriculum, is intended for more advanced managers. This differentiation will be discussed in greater detail later.

From fall 1983 through summer 1984, Sue R. Faerman and I had direct responsibility for the design and development of the two curricula. This was done in conjunction with a twenty-two person advisory group. Michael P. Thompson had administrative responsibility for the actual delivery and evaluation of the courses.

Design and Development of Two Parallel Curricula

If so small a change as altering a single course title in one academic department can be a difficult process, designing and writing an entire curriculum in an eight-month period, for delivery by fifteen different colleges and universities, might have seemed like an impossible task. First, no one school had a curriculum that matched that of any other school. Second, endless lists of unrelated skills existed in various needs assessments that had been performed by New York State. Third, similar lists of seemingly unrelated skills existed in the literature on managerial leadership (Livingston, 1971; Miner, 1973; Katz, 1974; Mintzberg, 1975; Cameron and Whetten, 1980; Yukl, 1981; Flanders, 1981; Boyatzis, 1982).

This latter point has led to some of the difficulty in arriving at a mutually acceptable concept of leadership (Korman, 1966; Miner, 1975; Salancik and others, 1975; Greene, 1977; Schriesheim and Kerr, 1977; Rosenbach and Taylor, 1984). In an attempt to integrate and organize the skills that would be suggested by the advisory group, it was proposed and agreed upon that the competing values framework be employed.

Design Process. The existence of an organizing framework provided a basic perceptual structure. The next step was to determine the structure for the courses comprising the two parallel curricula. This raised issues concerning the differing graduate course requirements across the various colleges and universities, the differentiation between the two curricula, and the relation between Public Service Training Program courses and existing departmental courses.

Each curriculum consists of four courses, corresponding to the four quadrants of the competing values framework. Each course is divided into two modules, corresponding to the two roles associated with each skill quadrant. Micro- and macro-organizational perspectives provide the basis for differentiating between the two curricula. That is, the curriculum developed for supervisors emphasizes a micro-organizational approach and focuses on individual performance factors; the curriculum developed for higher-level administrators emphasizes a macro-organizational approach and focuses on organizational performance factors.

The design of courses was initially set to follow the intensive modular format used in many colleges and universities that offer executive development programs for practicing managers. This format combines intensive in-class experience with guided independent study. Each course is built around six days of intensive class time that includes lectures, discussions, and group work (a day is defined as six hours of in-class experience). The six days are divided into two three-day modules. One month before beginning the first module, participants receive reading and, occasionally, writing assignments. Eleven days separate the two modules, providing time for participants to complete additional reading and writing assignments. Following the second module, participants complete a final assignment, usually involving on-the-job implementation of the concepts and skills acquired in class.

The twenty-two person advisory group, consisting of

eleven nationally recognized scholars and eleven prominent
state administrators and representatives of the Public Employees Federation, was assembled to identify specific skills to be
included in each course. Participants were chosen on the basis of
their experience and expertise in the field of management as
practitioners or scholars.

As the first step in the curriculum development process,
the team reviewed the existing literature and needs assessments
to identify an initial list of potential topic areas for each course.
Sample items from these lists were then chosen and sent to
members of the advisory committee, who were asked to review
the lists and also to suggest additional topics for inclusion in the
curricula. Over 250 potential topics were identified through this
questionnaire. Based on the responses, the curriculum development team organized a packet of materials to be distributed
when the committee convened. This packet consisted of a description of the theoretical framework and an outline of the
basic structure of the courses and modules to be designed,
including a description of the individual or organizational performance factors and a list of potential topics for each module.

Selecting Specific Skills. Given the difficult task of creating an
outline for each of the eight courses — an outline that was to
include topic areas and guidelines for the relative emphasis to
be given to the different topic areas — it was decided to use an
automated decision conference to design the eight courses.
Automated decision conferencing is a process that blends organization development and management science techniques to
help individuals and groups solve complex problems. (For an
extensive description see Quinn, Rohrbaugh, and McGrath,
1985.) Combining the expertise of group facilitators with state-
of-the-art computer software, automated decision conferencing
allows a group to consider even the most subjective aspects of a
decision, in a framework that focuses and clarifies group priorities. That is, rather than attempting to increase the objectivity of the decision makers' perspectives, this process allows
decision makers to surface values that drive arguments, consider
them in a consistent and coherent process, and make a decision

based on a mutual understanding of the group's priorities and a thorough consideration of all relevant factors.

The advisory committee was convened to participate in a two-day automated decision conference, made possible by the Decision Techtronics Group of Rockefeller College. The task was defined as a resource allocation problem, that is, a problem that requires the allocation of a limited resource, such as time, space, or money, across a number of possible purposes, uses, or activities, where the resource requirements of performing all possibilities far exceed the available resources. In this case, the resource of time had to be allocated across the different potential topic areas and activities associated with each topic.

The committee was divided into four subgroups. Each subgroup was then charged with the task of defining broad categories of instruction and describing incremental levels of instruction and learning activities in each category, where each incremental level reflected increased benefit and increased investment of time over the preceding one. Group members then assessed the overall benefit and cost in instruction time for each level and examined the relative benefit-cost ratios for including each of the different potential topic areas. At the end of the conference, each group was able to make final recommendations for the design of the courses, including the specific topic areas to be included, a suggested time allocation for each of these topic areas, and potential instruction and learning activities for each topic area.

Developing the Curricula. Using the design guidelines generated at the decision conference, curriculum writers worked intensively over the next eight months to develop the eight courses. They wrote brief course and module descriptions to correspond to the eight course outlines developed at the decision conference. These descriptions were then distributed to twelve departments of administration and management in New York State and to selected individuals nationwide. Each department or individual was asked to suggest potential case studies, group exercises, readings, and assignments based on the course descriptions.

It should be noted that each course corresponds to a quadrant in the competing values framework. Each module in the Program in Supervision corresponds to one of the eight leadership roles. Each module in the Program in Administration corresponds to a parallel organizational performance factor in the competing values framework of organizational effectiveness. For example, course 3 in the Program in Supervision is entitled "How to Work with Individuals and Groups." This course focuses on human relations skills, pictured in the upper-left quadrant of the framework. Module 1 includes the units "Increasing Sensitivity and Concern," "Counseling/Interviewing/ Listening," and "Performance Appraisal." These are skills associated with the role of "mentor." Module 2 includes the units "Team Building," "Participative Decision Making," and "Conflict Management." These are skills associated with the role of "group facilitator."

At the organizational level, course 3 of the Program in Administration is entitled "Essentials of Developing Human Resources." Again, this course focuses on the topic of human relations, but at a more macro level. Module 1 of this course is entitled "Human Systems," and it deals with topics associated with human resource development, training and development issues, affirmative action issues, and new trends in human resource management. Module 2 is entitled "Work Climate," and it covers topics associated with organizational culture, quality of work life, and other interventions into human systems. Figures 23 and 24 show the topics covered in each course of the Program in Supervision and the Program in Administration, respectively.

In each module, an adult education model developed by Whetten and Cameron (1984) was employed. This model suggests that skill development consists of five activities: skill assessment, skill learning, skill analysis, skill practice, and skill application.

Skill assessment involves paper-and-pencil instruments, awareness questions, attitude explorations, and other activities designed to assess the participant's level of knowledge and/or ability and to stimulate introspection and interest in the topic. Skill learning includes concepts, ideas, and skills selected for

Figure 23. Program in Supervision.

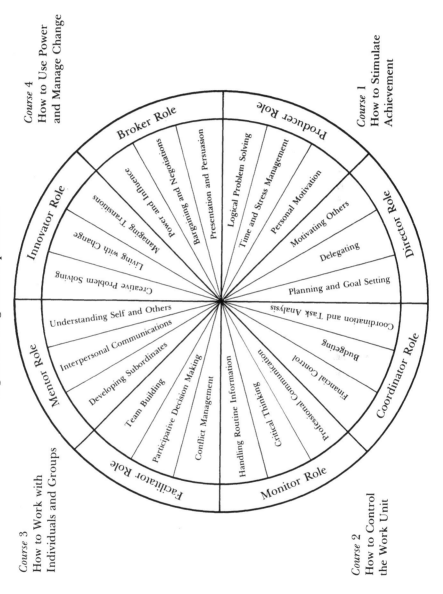

Figure 24. Program in Administration.

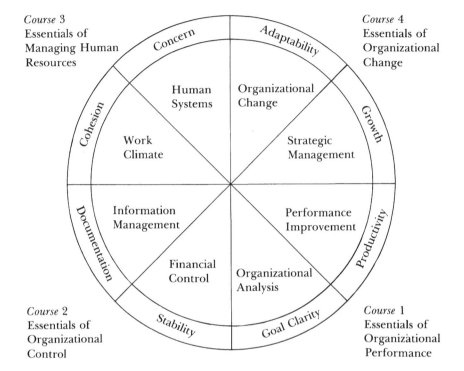

Course 3
Essentials of
Managing Human
Resources

Course 4
Essentials of
Organizational
Change

Course 2
Essentials of
Organizational
Control

Course 1
Essentials of
Organizational
Performance

presentation. Skill analysis contains case studies or other activities designed to stimulate the participant's critical analysis of how others act in certain situations. Skill practice consists of several exercises, case studies, and role plays that illustrate key concepts and allow participants to practice skills acquired in previous steps. Skill application consists of on-the-job implementation of principles and skills and is supplemented by instructor feedback on written assignments.

Issues in Implementation

By the spring of 1984 the first drafts of the Program in Supervision were ready for classroom testing. This marked the beginning of the implementation stage. This stage, however, was to be complicated by four major issues. First, the program was a statewide initiative requiring balanced levels of participation among the involved schools. Second, the potential participants were widely dispersed across the state and were eager to have courses in locations convenient to them. Third, each agency, whether large or small, wanted a "fair share" of the potential seats in each classroom. Fourth, each school had to offer credit and ensure that the curriculum was followed by the instructors. Given the purposes of this chapter, I will review the dynamics surrounding the last issue.

Standardization. A major reason for the development of the curriculum was the state government's desire for assurance that there would be an academically sound, applied curriculum taught to all participants. Regardless of the school offering the course, or the location in which it was taken, all participants were to receive the same basic instruction. Similarly, a project advisory committee, representing both state management and the union, wanted a curriculum that would (1) make a difference in the way people viewed their jobs and performed at work, and (2) have content that would be credit worthy at the best schools of management. The program was to be an initiative for both improving performance among state professionals (this would benefit the state) and providing professional development opportunities for individual participants (this would benefit the union). Ideally, each course would be applicable toward the M.P.A. degree through the school where it was offered. For these reasons, a fairly strict set of procedures was imposed.

Many of the schools had members of their faculty on the curriculum development advisory group. This was, for the most part, a very positive factor when the time came for a department or school to approve the use of the curriculum through some kind of formal governance process. Most departments were willing to "test" the curriculum and to offer graduate credit for it.

One of the most controversial issues to emerge at this point was the question of standardization. While some faculty members welcomed new material, organized in a coherent design, others were upset by the need to adhere to the curriculum. They were, in essence, being asked to teach a course that they had not designed. Hence, some people saw the program as an imposition, an inappropriate constraint on academic freedom.

The strongest complaints were raised against the use of skill-based, experiential teaching methods. Some faculty members argued that the program consisted of training modules rather than academic courses. These reactions stimulated some provocative discussions about professional education, management skill development, and the role of universities in preparing managers. In some cases, objections were answered by enhancing course content, that is, by adding additional required readings or assignments that instructors felt were essential for credit-bearing courses.

Over time much of the resistance subsided. Even many of the instructors who initially opposed the program agreed to experiment with it. Most of the time this led to a change in outlook. Below are two statements taken from evaluations by instructors who had been extremely resistant to the program at the outset. According to the first instuctor, "We haven't taught many of these things in our department because we deal more with theory than administrative practice. It was refreshing to get in the trenches with these people and deal with real strategies and reactions." The second wrote, "Our bias in academia is often against the useful and the specific. We sometimes hide behind theory and generalization. I've enjoyed working through this material with people who make their living doing what we claim we're preparing our graduates to do."

Content. While most of the resistance centered on the use of skill-based, experiential methods, the specific content of the curricula also raised some issues. For example, one month before the first offering of the course entitled "Organizational Control" was to begin, two instructors who were to team-teach the course told their dean that they would not teach it unless certain modifications were made in the curriculum. They wanted more emphasis on certain issues in finance and budgeting and less emphasis on other topics. It was agreed to carry out the suggested changes and make both versions of the curriculum available. As other faculty in several schools began teaching the same course, they were almost equally divided on which of the two versions was preferable.

Diversity. Another challenge for faculty was the way in which the topics in each of the courses were arranged. Each course had combinations of topics not usually found in "traditional" curricula. For example, the supervision course, "How to Understand and Control the Work Unit," included such topics as handling routine information, thinking critically, technical writing, financial control in the work unit, essentials of budgeting, and task analysis. These topics not only are seldom combined in a single course but also represent special skills and expertise usually not possessed by a single instructor. Many of the courses needed to be team taught by two instructors. Most students felt that this was an added benefit, but in a few cases instructors failed to maintain continuity and uniform standards.

Complementarity. Another issue was that of complementarity with existing curricula. The program was under such intense pressure to design and deliver the courses that there was not sufficient time for academic departments to create new course numbers and titles for these special courses and take them through a college or campuswide governance process. In the first semester, therefore, departments often attached special topics numbers to them and ran them as experimental courses. Occasionally, departments offered them under the titles and numbers of courses in the "traditional" curriculum that were most like them.

Soon, these short-term solutions began giving way to inevitable questions such as: Should the original course now be changed to match what is offered through the Public Service Training Program? Do we accept these courses as filling requirements toward graduate degrees? If not, why not? Clearly, the large number of participants in the Public Service Training Program courses seemed to prefer the newly designed courses to the more traditional ones. Throughout the first year, there were occasionally complaints from students that schools were not offering the new courses as they were designed in the syllabi and that instead instructors were teaching the "same old courses" that had always been in the bulletins. However, the more faculty worked with the new syllabi, the more comfortable they seemed to feel in using them, and the more comfortable were faculty committees and departments with the proposed idea of offering a statewide certificate in advanced public management.

Implications for Increased Effectiveness

The curriculum is skill focused and is based on a systematic theoretical framework. Let us consider each of these characteristics and their implications for the development of management education programs.

With its systematic use of skill-based learning methodologies, the program gives participants the traditional conceptual basis for learning, but goes beyond this by forcing them to apply the acquired concepts and skills both in the classroom and on the job. The final assignment for each course requires that particpants return to their jobs and implement one of the concepts learned in class. In asking the participants to "learn by doing" rather than "understand by listening," the program has begun to bridge the gap between administration as an academic discipline and administration as a professional practice. In essence, the program not only tells the little girl how to ride a bicycle it also helps her to try riding one.

While preliminary classroom evaluations from students are very positive, the question remains as to the impact of the program on behavior. A major, systematic evaluation of this question has been funded by New York State and is being directed by Sue R. Faerman. A central question in her analysis will be the match between an individual's personal style and his or her development of skills. More specifically, how does skill development take place in a person's stronger quadrants when compared with their weaker quadrants? Her research promises to be most interesting.

Conclusion:
Beyond Rational Management

One thesis of this book is that managers can make the journey from novice to master. In so doing, they undergo some profound changes. The journey begins firmly rooted in the purposive frame that is reflected in the two models in the bottom half of the competing values framework. People who use this frame are very good at setting goals, evaluating alternatives, and proceeding in a logical way. In this frame the emphasis is on rules and discipline.

Management theory, formal and informal, tends to reflect the logic of the novice. It is based on hierarchical logic and is filled with rules of action. The problem is that as individuals come to better understand the dynamic world of real organizations, they also discover that these rules are insufficient and limiting. They learn to see their world in more dynamic, holistic, and intuitive ways. They discover the difference between the map and the territory.

Seeing holistically sometimes helps people to reframe their problems and to create states of high performance. They experience what we have called "flow." The whole becomes greater than the sum of its parts. People become highly energized and capable of extraordinary achievements. In this state, time seems to stop and communication takes place at a level beyond words. Dualities and dichotomies disappear as polarities become one. Great insight, understanding, and unity emerge.

When people, afterwards, try to explain this experience, they often have great difficulty in doing so. Language is a sequential tool. Its causal structure invariably distorts the holistic reality of the flow experience. Written and verbal descriptions are always an approximation at best. Written theories, for the most part, take us away from, rather than toward, individual mastery and collective excellence. We forget that the map is not the territory; we mistake the word for the thing.

People have biases in the way they process information. Some are very predisposed to the purposive frame (bottom half), others to the holistic frame (top half). Within these two broad frames are the quadrants of the competing values framework, and here too people are predisposed to the assumptions of one quadrant over another. Particular ways of organizing and leading are seen as morally right or wrong. People cannot easily see the strengths and the weaknesses in each of the quadrants or in each of the two frames.

The result of this information-processing bias is that people have a tendency to create negative space. They pursue the values in a given quadrant until a strange loop occurs. The positive value becomes negative. This incomprehensible event often places people in a vicious circle where they keep accelerating their commitment to the value that is causing their problem in the first place (Quinn and Cameron, 1988). This problem characterizes the purposive sense-making experiences of both practitioners and scholars and is reflected in the theories of both.

People who are predisposed to the purposive frame, like the engineer in Chapter One, find the assumptions of the top two quadrants difficult to comprehend. As they move into increasingly complex and dynamic situations, their perceptions of reality become increasingly distorted. People who are predisposed to the holistic frame have the opposite problem. Like Don Burr at People Express, they strive for constant change, growth, stimulation, and reframing. They seek, at all costs, to stop the charismatic system from moving to a routinized state. They negatively define the assumptions of the bottom two quadrants.

Some people, like Bill Gates at Microsoft, seem to have the ability to use more frames than others do. As situations change, they adjust their operating assumptions accordingly. The masters in Chapter Seven, for example, are seen as being able to operate at a high level in all four quadrants. Ineffective managers, however, tended to be badly out of balance. Master managers have the capacity to engage in what Torbert (1987) calls *action inquiry*, that is, they have the ability to take action and to inquire at the same time. They simultaneously use multiple frames, and this allows them to more frequently take advantage of the moment. Becoming a master manager is not easy. It involves a long career of painful learning. However, by making explicit the differences and the complementarities in the competing values framework, people can become aware of that which is often missed entirely in the course of some careers. Making the competing positive tensions in management explicit is the first way that this book can be helpful.

In the course of the book, I also offer a three-step process for self-improvement. This process has aided a number of people to understand and improve themselves. In addition, a number of tools that might assist a person in the improvement process are provided. Finally, this book describes a major program designed to develop skills and provide a more complex understanding of the paradoxes and competing demands of organizational life. I hope that the description will be of assistance to those who design management programs for others.

Unifying Polarities

In closing, let me further define what it means to move beyond rational management. Moving beyond rational management does not mean moving from the purposive to the holistic frame. It does not mean moving from Theory X to Theory Y or from a left- to a right-brain perspective. It does not in any way mean devaluing rational thinking.

A key point is the difference between the purposive (bottom half) and holistic (top half) frames. The purposive frame is based on either/or logic and is hence always excluding things. One thing that is excluded is the holistic frame. Either the world is real, tangible, and practical or it is mysterious, intangible, and soft. Since it is clearly the first, it cannot be the second. In contrast, the logic of the holistic frame is inclusive. The key insight is that while the purposive frame excludes the holistic, the holistic frame includes the purposive. Hence, it is possible to be both holistic and purposive. Here we are suggesting a frame that integrates rather than differentiates the elements of the competing values framework. Gawain (1982) illustrates how both the purposive and holistic frames operate together in the following metaphor:

"Let us imagine that life is a river. Most people are cling- ing to the bank, afraid to let go and risk being carried along by the current of the river. At a certain point, each person must be willing to simply let go, and trust the river to carry him or her along safely. At this point he learns to 'go with the flow' and it feels wonderful.

"Once he has gotten used to being in the flow of the river, he can begin to look ahead and guide his own course onward, deciding where the course looks best, steering his way around boulders and snags, and choosing which of the many channels and branches of the river he prefers to follow, all the while still 'going with the flow'" (p. 29).

The purposive frame keeps people clinging to the bank. In order to enter the holistic frame, they must let go. In the holistic frame, however, they continue to use the purposive frame. The first step of development is to experience the holistic frame. The problem, however, is that people who come to know and value the holistic frame almost always lose its inclusiveness. They take a purposive perspective on holism and choose to see the two perspectives from an either/or point of view. They there- fore resist returning to the purposive frame. This becomes a problem in both practice and in theory building.

Moving beyond rational management means using both frames. It means moving through three steps. The first step is recognizing polarities. The second step is seeing the strength and the weaknesses in each of the polar perspectives. The third, and most challenging, step is not to affix to one or the other but to move to a metalevel that allows one to see the interpenetra- tion and the inseparability of the two polarities. This third step takes us to a transformational logic. It allows for simultaneous integration and differentiation. It allows us to understand management at a deeper, more complex and dynamic, level—the level of the master.

Conclusion

Neither our current theories nor our schools of management are oriented to developing the capacities outlined above. The research discussed earlier suggests that the development of mastery comes through painful experience and is achieved by only a small minority of all managers. Those who develop mastery have the capacity to balance polarities in a way that is difficult for theorists or practitioners to describe.

In conclusion, then, moving beyond rational management means moving to a metalevel that allows one to tolerate, consider, and employ both the purposive and holistic frames. It means simultaneously using multiple frames to more effectively function in a world of paradox and competing demands.

Resource A:
A Competing Values Reading List

This resource contains a reading list organized according to the competing values framework and designed to help you identify books that address the areas in which you need improvement. It is meant to suggest a few of the many readings that can expand your knowledge in each area. Readers are encouraged to send the author additional suggestions of books for inclusion.

Facilitator Role

Beck, A. C., and Hillmar, E. D. *Positive Management Practices: Bringing Out the Best in Organizations and People.* San Francisco: Jossey-Bass, 1986.

Blake, R., Mouton, J., and Allen, R. *Spectacular Teamwork: What It Is, How to Recognize It, How to Bring It About.* New York: Wiley, 1987.

Doyle, D. S. *How to Make Meetings Work.* New York: Jove, 1982.

Dyer, W. G. *Team Building.* Reading, Mass.: Addison-Wesley, 1987.

Filley, A. C. *Interpersonal Conflict Resolution.* Glenview, Ill.: Scott, Foresman, 1975.

Fox, W. M. *Effective Group Problem Solving: How to Broaden Participation, Improve Decision Making, and Increase Commitment to Action.* San Francisco: Jossey-Bass, 1987.

Janis, I. *Victims of Groupthink.* Boston: Houghton Mifflin, 1972.

Lawler, E. E. III. *High-Involvement Management: Participative Strategies for Improving Organizational Performance.* San Francisco: Jossey-Bass, 1986.

Ouchi, W. G. *Theory Z: How American Business Can Meet the Japanese Challenge.* Reading, Mass.: Addison-Wesley, 1981.

Walton, R. E. *Managing Conflict: Interpersonal Dialogue and Third-Party Roles.* (2nd ed.) Reading, Mass.: Addison-Wesley, 1987.

Zander, A. *Making Groups Effective.* San Francisco: Jossey-Bass, 1982.

Zander, A. *The Purposes of Groups and Organizations.* San Francisco: Jossey-Bass, 1985.

Mentor Role

Carnegie, D., and Carnegie, D. *How to Win Friends and Influence People.* New York: Simon & Schuster, 1981.

Drake, J. D. *Effective Interviewing: A Guide for Managers.* New York: AMACOM, 1972.

Hall, D. T. *Careers in Organization.* Pacific Palisades, Calif.: Goodyear, 1976.

Helmstetter, S. *What to Say When You Talk to Yourself.* New York: Pocket Books, 1986.

James, M., and Jongewood, D. *Born to Win.* Reading, Mass.: Addison-Wesley, 1977.

Kotter, J., Faux, V. A., and McArthur, C. C. *Self-Assessment and Career Development.* Englewood Cliffs, N.J.: Prentice-Hall, 1978.

McGregor, D. *The Human Side of Enterprise.* New York: McGraw-Hill, 1960.

Maslow, A. *Motivation and Personality.* (2nd ed.) New York: Harper & Row, 1970.

Nierenberg, G. I., and Calero, H. H. *How to Read a Person Like a Book.* New York: Pocket Books, 1973.

Progoff, I. *At a Journal Workshop: The Basic Text and Guide for Using the Intensive Journal.* New York: Dialogue House Library, 1975.

Reece, B. L., and Brandt, R. *Effective Human Relations in Business.* Boston: Houghton Mifflin, 1981.

Rogers, C. R. *On Becoming a Person.* Boston: Houghton Mifflin, 1961.

Rogers, C. R., and Stevens, B. *Person to Person: The Problem of Being Human.* Lafayette, Calif.: Real People Press, 1967.

Rusk, T., and Reed, R. *I Want to Change but I Don't Know How.* Los Angeles: Price/Stern/Sloan, 1986.

Schein, E. H. *Career Dynamics: Matching Individual and Organizational Needs.* Reading, Mass.: Addison-Wesley, 1978.

Sheehy, G. *Passages: Predictable Crises of Adult Life.* New York: Dutton, 1976.

Sher, B. *Wishcraft: How to Get What You Really Want.* New York: Ballantine, 1983.

Torbert, W. R. *Managing the Corporate Dream: Restructuring for Long-Term Success.* Homewood, Ill.: Dow Jones-Irwin, 1987.

Innovator Role

Ackoff, R. L. *The Art of Problem Solving.* New York: Wiley, 1987.

Albrecht, K. *The Creative Corporation.* Homewood, Ill.: Dow Jones-Irwin, 1987.

Beckhard, R., and Harris, R. T. *Organizational Transitions.* (2nd ed.) Reading, Mass.: Addison-Wesley, 1987.

Brandt, S. C. *Entrepreneuring in Established Companies: Managing Toward the Year 2000.* New York: Mentor, 1986.

Hornstein, H. A. *Managerial Courage.* New York: Wiley, 1986.

Kanter, R. M. *The Change Masters: Innovation for Productivity in the American Corporation.* New York: Simon & Schuster, 1983.

Keil, J. M. *The Creative Mystique: How to Manage It, Nurture It, and Make It Pay.* New York: Wiley, 1985.

Kilmann, R. H. *Beyond the Quick Fix: Managing Five Tracks to Organizational Success.* San Francisco: Jossey-Bass, 1984.

Kirkpatrick, D. L. *How to Manage Change Effectively: Approaches, Methods, and Case Examples.* San Francisco: Jossey-Bass, 1985.

LeBoeuf, M. *Imagineering: How to Profit from Your Creative Powers.* New York: Berkley Book, 1980.

Martel, L. *Mastering Change: The Key to Business Success.* New York: Simon & Schuster, 1986.

Nayak, P. R., and Kettersingham, J. M. *Break-Through.* New York: Rawson Associates, 1986.

Peale, N. V. *The Power of Positive Thinking.* New York: Fawcett Books, 1956.

Pinchot, G. III. *Intrapreneuring: Why You Don't Have to Leave the*

Corporation to Become an Entrepreneur. New York: Harper & Row, 1985.

Ray, M., and Myers, R. *Creativity in Business.* New York: Doubleday, 1986.

Shakt, G. *Creative Visualization.* New York: Bantam Books, 1978.

Tichy, N. M. *Managing Strategic Change: Organization Development Redefined.* New York: Wiley, 1983.

Tichy, N. M., and Devanna, M. A. *The Transformational Leader.* New York: Wiley, 1986.

Von Oech, R. *A Whack on the Side of the Head: How to Unlock Your Mind for Innovation.* New York: Warner Books, 1983.

Von Oech, R. *A Kick in the Seat of the Pants: Using Your Explorer, Artist, Judge, and Warrior to Be More Creative.* New York: Harper & Row, 1986.

Broker Role

Allen, R. W., and Porter, L. W. *Organizational Influence Processes.* Glenview, Ill.: Scott, Foresman, 1983.

Back, K., and Back, K. *Assertiveness at Work: A Practical Guide to Handling Awkward Situations.* New York: McGraw-Hill, 1982.

Bedrosian, M. M. *Speak Like a Pro: Building Visibility, Impact, and Profits Through Public Speaking.* New York: Wiley, 1987.

Block, P. *The Empowered Manager: Positive Political Skills at Work.* San Francisco: Jossey-Bass, 1987.

Cohen, H. *You Can Negotiate Anything: How to Get What You Want.* New York: Bantam, 1982.

Culbert, S., and McDonald, J. J. *Radical Management: Power Politics and the Pursuit of Trust.* New York: Free Press, 1985.

Fisher, R., and Ury, W. *Getting to Yes: Negotiating Agreement Without Giving In.* New York: Viking Penguin, 1983.

Greenburger, F., and Kiernan, T. *How to Ask for More and Get It: The Art of Creative Negotiation.* New York: Doubleday, 1978.

Hegarty, C. *How to Manage Your Boss.* New York: Ballantine, 1982.

Jandt, F. E. *Win-Win Negotiating: Turning Conflict into Agreement.* New York: Wiley, 1985.

Kenny, M. *Presenting Yourself.* New York: Wiley, 1982.

Korda, M. *Power: How to Get It, How to Use It.* New York: Random House, 1975.

Leech, T. *How to Prepare, Stage, and Deliver Winning Presentations.* New York: AMACOM, 1982.

Nirenberg, J. S. *How to Sell Your Ideas.* New York: McGraw-Hill, 1984.

Pfeifter, J. *Power in Organizations.* Marshfield, Mass.: Pitman, 1981.

Smith, M. J. *When I Say No, I Feel Guilty.* New York: Bantam Books, 1975.

Viscott, D. *Winning.* New York: Pocket Books, 1987.

Yates, D. T., Jr. *The Politics of Management: Exploring the Inner Workings of Public and Private Organizations.* San Francisco: Jossey-Bass, 1985.

Director Role

Albrecht, K. *Successful Management by Objectives: An Action Manual.* Englewood Cliffs, N.J.: Prentice-Hall, 1978.

Allison, G. T. *Essence of Decision: Explaining the Cuban Missile Crisis.* Boston: Little, Brown, 1971.

Behn, R. D., and Vaupel J. W. *Quick Analysis for Busy Decision Makers.* New York: Basic Books, 1982.

Below, P. J., Morrisey, G. L., and Acomb, B. L. *The Executive Guide to Strategic Planning.* San Francisco: Jossey-Bass, 1987.

Benson, H., and Kipper, M. Z. *The Relaxation Response.* New York: Avon Books, 1975.

Drucker, P. F., *Managing for Results: Economic Tasks and Risk-Taking Decisions.* New York: Harper & Row, 1964.

Engel, H. M. *How to Delegate: A Guide to Getting Things Done.* Houston, Tex.: Gulf, 1983.

Huber, G. P. *Managerial Decision Making.* Glenview, Ill.: Scott, Foresman, 1986.

Jenks, J. M., and Kelly, J. M. *Don't Do. Delegate!* New York: Ballantine, 1985.

Keppner, C. H., and Tregoe, B. B. *The Rational Manager: A Systematic Approach to Problem Solving and Decision Making.* New York: McGraw-Hill, 1965.

Mali, P. *MBO Updated: A Handbook of Practices and Techniques for Managing Objectives.* New York: Wiley, 1986.

Selye, H. *The Stress of Life* (2nd ed.) New York: McGraw-Hill, 1978.

Woolfolk, R. L., and Richardson, F. C. *Stress, Sanity, and Survival.* New York: New American Library, 1979.

Producer Role

Bain, D. *The Productivity Prescription: The Manager's Guide to Improving Productivity and Profits.* New York: McGraw-Hill, 1982.

Friedman, M. *Overcoming the Fear of Success: Why and How We Defeat Ourselves and What to Do About It.* New York: Warner Books, 1980.

Grove, A. S. *High-Output Management.* New York: Random House, 1985.

Kendrick, J. W. *Improving Company Productivity.* Baltimore, Md.: Johns Hopkins University Press, 1984.

Kushel, G. *The Fully Effective Executive.* Chicago: Contemporary Books, 1983.

Mandell, M. *1001 Ways to Operate Your Business More Profitably.* Homewood, Ill.: Dow Jones-Irwin, 1975.

Nash, M. *Managing Organizational Performance.* San Francisco: Jossey-Bass, 1983.

Nash, M. *Making People Productive: What Really Works in Raising Managerial and Employee Performance.* San Francisco: Jossey-Bass, 1985.

Phillips, J. J. *Improving Supervisors' Effectiveness: How Organizations Can Raise the Performance of Their First-Level Managers.* San Francisco: Jossey-Bass, 1985.

Sawyer, G. C. *Designing Strategy.* New York: Wiley, 1986.

Stankard, M. F. *Productivity by Choice: The 20 to 1 Principle.* New York: Wiley, 1986.

Vough, C. F. *Productivity: A Practical Program for Improving Efficiency.* New York: AMACOM, 1979.

Ziglar, Z. *Top Performance: How to Develop Excellence in Yourself and Others.* New York: Berkley Book, 1986.

Monitor Role

Adler, M., and Van Doren, C. *How to Read a Book.* New York: Simon & Schuster, 1972.

Brown, A. S. *Maximizing Memory Power: Using Recall to Your Advantage in Business.* New York: Wiley, 1987.

Cascio, W. F. *Costing Human Resources: The Financial Impact of Behavior in Organizations.* New York: Van Nostrand Reinhold, 1982.

Eisenberg, R. *Organize Yourself.* New York: Macmillan, 1986.

Fockart, J., and Delong, D. W. *Executive Support Systems: The Myth and Reality of Top Management Computer Use.* Homewood, Ill.: Dow Jones-Irwin, 1987.

Posner, M. J. *Executive Essentials. Part II: Coping with the Information Explosion.* New York: Avon Books, 1982.

Reimold, C. *How to Write a Million-Dollar Memo.* New York: Dell, 1984.

Salerno, L. M. (ed.). "Catching Up with the Computer Revolution." *Harvard Business Review Executive Book Series*, New York: Wiley, 1983.

Sloma, R. S. *How to Measure Managerial Performance.* New York: Macmillan, 1980.

Winston, S. *The Organized Executive: New Ways to Manage Time, Paper, and People.* New York: Norton, 1983.

Coordinator Role

Becker, F. *The Successful Office: How to Create a Workspace That Is Right for You.* Reading, Mass.: Addison-Wesley, 1982.

Bernstein, L. A. *Analysis of Financial Statements.* Homewood, Ill.: Dow Jones-Irwin, 1984.

Drucker, P. F. *Management: Tasks, Responsibilities, and Practices.* New York: Harper & Row, 1973.

Frame, J. D. *Managing Projects in Organizations: How to Make the Best Use of Time, Techniques, and People.* San Francisco: Jossey-Bass, 1987.

Kish, J. L., Jr. *Office Management Problem Solver.* Radnor, Pa.: Chilton, 1983.

Loen, R. O. *Manage More by Doing Less.* New York: McGraw-Hill, 1971.

Newman, W. H. *Constructive Control: Design and Use of Control Systems.* Englewood Cliffs, N.J.: Prentice-Hall, 1975.

Nickerson, C. B. *The Accounting Handbook for Non-Accountants.* Boston: CBI Publishing, 1975.

Oncken, W. *Managing Management Time: Who's Got the Monkey?* Englewood Cliffs, N.J.: Prentice-Hall, 1984.

Vollmann, T. E., Berry, W. L., and Whybark, D. C. *Manufacturing Planning and Control Systems.* Homewood, Ill.: Dow Jones-Irwin, 1987.

Wanat, J. *Introduction to Budgeting.* Boston: Duxbury Press, 1978.

Winston, S. *The Organized Executive: New Ways to Manage Time, Paper, and People.* New York: Norton, 1983.

Resource B:
Competing Values
Leadership Instrument:
Extended Version

Following is the extended version of the competing values leadership instrument presented in Chapter Nine. The instrument is presented first. In its present form, it asks respondents to indicate (1) how frequently the manager engages in each behavior at the present time and (2) how frequently the manager should engage in each behavior.

The instrument is followed by an item key. The item key reflects a recent analysis in which over six hundred subordinates in the utility industry described their immediate superiors. Reliabilities are shown for each scale. A factor analysis, with an equamax rotation, was performed on the items after partialing out the effects of halo. The analysis produced eight factors. The factor variance and item loadings are presented. In addition, several new or modified items are indicated. It should be noted that in this instrument the focus of the producer items shifts from a more personal to a more managerial orientation.

On the same sample, a second version of the instrument, here labeled the "Competing Values Managerial Skills Instrument," was also tested. The same data are presented.

Exhibit 10. Competing Values Instrument: Managerial Leadership (Extended Version)

Listed here are some behaviors that a manager might employ. Using the following scale, please indicate the frequency with which each one is now used, as well as the frequency with which it should be used.

1. Almost never		5. Frequently
2. Very seldom	4. Occasionally	6. Very frequently
3. Seldom		7. Almost always

	Freq. Does This Now	*Freq. Should Do This*
1. Comes up with inventive ideas	____	____
2. Protects continuity in day-to-day operations	____	____
3. Exerts upward influence in the organization	____	____
4. Carefully reviews detailed reports	____	____
5. Maintains a "results" orientation in the unit	____	____
6. Facilitates consensus building in the work unit	____	____
7. Defines areas of responsibility for subordinates	____	____
8. Listens to the personal problems of subordinates	____	____
9. Minimizes disruptions to the work flow	____	____
10. Experiments with new concepts and procedures	____	____
11. Encourages participative decision making in the group	____	____
12. Makes sure everyone knows where the unit is going	____	____
13. Influences decisions made at higher levels	____	____
14. Compares records, reports, and so on to detect discrepancies	____	____
15. Sees that the unit delivers on stated goals	____	____
16. Shows empathy and concern in dealing with subordinates	____	____
17. Works with technical information	____	____
18. Gets access to people at higher levels	____	____
19. Sets clear objectives for the work unit	____	____
20. Treats each individual in a sensitive, caring way	____	____
21. Keeps track of what goes on inside the unit	____	____
22. Does problem solving in creative, clever ways	____	____
23. Pushes the unit to meet objectives	____	____
24. Encourages subordinates to share ideas in the group	____	____
25. Searches for innovations and potential improvements	____	____

26. Clarifies priorities and direction   ____   ____
27. Persuasively sells new ideas to higher-ups   ____   ____
28. Brings a sense of order into the unit   ____   ____
29. Shows concern for the needs of subordinates   ____   ____
30. Emphasizes unit's achievement of stated purposes   ____   ____
31. Builds teamwork among group members   ____   ____
32. Analyzes written plans and schedules   ____   ____

Item Key
(with Alpha Scores, Factor Variance, and Item Loadings)

		Item Loadings
1.	Innovator (Alpha = .90; Factor Variance = 2.24)	
1.	Comes up with inventive ideas	(.69)
10.	Experiments with new concepts and procedures	(.67)
22.	Does problem solving in creative, clever ways	(.70)
25.	Searches for innovations and potential improvements	(.66)
2.	Broker (Alpha = .85; Factor Variance = 1.94)	
3.	Exerts upward influence in the organization	(.64)
13.	Influences decisions made at higher levels	(.70)
18.	Gets access to people at higher levels	(.52)
27.	Persuasively sells new ideas to higher-ups	(.64)
3.	Producer (Alpha = .72; Factor Variance = 1.37)	
5.	Maintains a "results" orientation in the unit	(.58)
15.	Sees that the unit delivers on stated goals	(.52)
*23.	Pushes the unit to meet objectives	
*30.	Emphasizes unit's achievement of stated purposes	
4.	Director (Alpha = .79; Factor Variance = 1.52)	
7.	Defines areas of responsibility for subordinates	(.54)

    12.   Makes sure everyone knows where the unit
           is going   (.51)
    19.   Sets clear objectives for the work unit   (.49)
  *26.   Clarifies priorities and direction
5.   Coordinator (Alpha = .77; Factor Variance = 1.29)
    2.   Protects continuity in day-to-day
        operations   (.43)
    9.   Minimizes disruptions to the work flow   (.40)
    21.   Keeps track of what goes on inside the
         unit   (.56)
  **28.   Brings a sense of order into the unit   (.48)
6.   Monitor (Alpha = .73; Factor Variance = 1.54)
    4.   Carefully reviews detailed reports   (.67)
    14.   Compares records, reports, and so on to
         detect discrepancies   (.69)
    17.   Works with technical information   (.49)
  *32.   Analyzes written plans and schedules
7.   Facilitator (Alpha = .89; Factor Variance = 2.07)
    6.   Facilitates consensus building in the work
        unit   (.54)
    11.   Encourages participative decision making
         in the group   (.63)
    24.   Encourages subordinates to share ideas in
         the group   (.63)
    31.   Builds teamwork among group members   (.54)
8.   Mentor (Alpha = .87; Factor Variance = 2.13)
    8.   Listens to the personal problems of
        subordinates   (.64)
    16.   Shows empathy and concern in dealing
         with subordinates   (.75)
    20.   Treats each individual in a sensitive,
         caring way   (.71)
  **29.   Shows concern for the needs of
        subordinates   (.40)

---

* New item since last analysis
** Wording modified since last analysis

Exhibit 11. Competing Values Managerial Skills Instrument.

Listed here are some behaviors that a manager might employ. Using the following scale, please indicate the frequency with which each one is now used, as well as the frequency with which it should be used.

1. Almost never		5. Frequently
2. Very seldom	4. Occasionally	6. Very frequently
3. Seldom		7. Almost always

	Extent Person Does This Now	Extent Person Should Do This
Encouraging innovation	1. ____	2. ____
Doing paper work	3. ____	4. ____
Working with facts	5. ____	6. ____
Mentoring/developing people	7. ____	8. ____
Increasing unit output	9. ____	10. ____
Resolving conflict in groups	11. ____	12. ____
Selling ideas	13. ____	14. ____
Conveying clear direction	15. ____	16. ____
Creative thinking	17. ____	18. ____
Technical analysis	19. ____	20. ____
Influencing upward	21. ____	22. ____
Reviewing/evaluating reports	23. ____	24. ____
Stimulating extra effort	25. ____	26. ____
Consensus building	27. ____	28. ____
Clarifying priorities	29. ____	30. ____
Listening to individuals	31. ____	32. ____
Writing budgets	33. ____	34. ____
Introducing change	35. ____	36. ____
Factual recall	37. ____	38. ____
Showing concern for people	39. ____	40. ____
Directing work efforts	41. ____	42. ____
Influencing peers	43. ____	44. ____
Maintaining productivity	45. ____	46. ____
Facilitating discussions	47. ____	48. ____
Logical problem solving	49. ____	50. ____
Understanding individuals	51. ____	52. ____
Providing new vision	53. ____	54. ____
Writing plans and schedules	55. ____	56. ____
Running cohesive meetings	57. ____	58. ____
Specifying purposes, reasons	59. ____	60. ____
Maintaining a power base	61. ____	62. ____
Achieving unit goals	63. ____	64. ____

Item Key
(with Alpha Scores, Factor Variance, and Item Loadings)

		Item Loadings
1.	Facilitator (Alpha = .81; Factor Variance = 1.92)	
11.	Resolving conflict in groups	(.56)
27.	Group consensus building	(.40)
47.	Facilitating group discussions	(.43)
57.	Running cohesive meetings	(.57)
2.	Mentor (Alpha = .88; Factor Variance = 2.57)	
7.	Mentoring/developing people	(.56)
31.	Listening to individuals	(.70)
39.	Showing concern for people	(.78)
51.	Understanding individuals	(.76)
3.	Innovator (Alpha = .86; Factor Variance = 2.32)	
1.	Encouraging innovation	(.57)
17.	Creative thinking	(.60)
35.	Introducing change	(.58)
53.	Providing new vision	(.68)
4.	Broker (Alpha = .81; Factor Variance = 2.12)	
13.	Selling ideas	(.66)
21.	Influencing upward	(.69)
43.	Influencing peers	(.54)
61.	Maintaining a power base	(.49)
5.	Producer (Alpha = .85; Factor Variance = 2.05)	
9.	Increasing unit output	(.63)
*25.	Stimulating extra effort	
45.	Maintaining productivity	(.56)
63.	Achieving unit goals	(.56)
6.	Director (Alpha = .83; Factor Variance = 1.98)	
15.	Conveying clear direction	(.59)
29.	Clarifying priorities	(.53)
**41.	Directing work efforts	(.53)
*59.	Specifying objectives	
7.	Coordinator (Alpha = .76; Factor Variance = 1.90)	
3.	Doing paper work	(.55)
**23.	Reviewing/evaluating reports	(.59)

**33.   Writing/reviewing budgets   (.46)
 *55.   Writing plans and schedules
8.   Monitor (Alpha = .89; Factor Variance = 2.42)
   5.   Working with facts   (.62)
  19.   Technical analysis   (.68)
  37.   Factual recall   (.58)
  49.   Logical problem solving   (.61)

 * New item
** Wording modified

Resource C:
Interview Questions for
Doing a Competing Values
Organizational Analysis

This resource contains a list of interview questions. Questions selected from the list can be used to guide qualitative studies of the four quadrants of the competing values framework.

**Exhibit 12. Interview Questions Based on the
Competing Values Approach.**

Introduction: Clarifying Comments and General Business

Do you understand why I am here?

Purpose: (1) obtain clarity

(2) ensure confidentiality

General Introductory Questions

1. I would like to know about your job — can you help me understand what you do on the job?

2. What is it like to work in this unit? How do you feel about working here?

3. How do others feel about working here?

4. Have things always been the way they are now?

Human Relations Model

1. How easy is it to find people to work in this unit?

2. How are people selected for jobs in this unit? (What procedures and criteria are used?)

3. How long do people stay in their jobs? (Why?)

4. When a person starts a new job here, what help is received?

5. Over time, what training and educational opportunities are made available?

6. In terms of job performance, how does a person know if he or she is doing well?

7. What are the most important rewards and benefits that people receive here?

8. How much cooperation and teamwork exist in this unit?

9. Overall, how much commitment do people have to their jobs?

Internal Process Model

1. What is the work flow like in this unit? (Where do you get your work from, and where does it go when you have finished with it?)

2. How is the work flow coordinated?

3. Does the work flow ever get disrupted? (When?) (How?) (How often?)

4. What are the most critical kinds of decisions made in this unit? How are they made?

5. What are the most common formal communication problems?

6. Do you do the same kind of work in the same manner every day, or does your work constantly change?

7. How much emphasis is placed on rules and procedures in the unit?

8. How significant or important is "automation" in your unit?

9. Overall, how efficient is your unit?

Rational Goal Model

1. What kind of planning takes place in the unit?

2. In planning your own work, do you need to think in terms of hours, days, weeks, months, or years?

3. What are the objectives of this unit?

4. Does everyone agree on what these objectives are?

5. Do these objectives ever change? (Why?) (How often?)

6. How intense is the work effort?

7. Overall, how productive is this unit?

Open Systems Model

1. Of the various outside demands that are made on this unit, which are the most critical?

2. How predictable are those demands? Are they always the same, or are they always changing?

3. How flexible is the unit, that is, how well does the unit adjust to changes? (Can you give some recent examples?)

4. What do outsiders think about this unit? What is its image or reputation?

5. From what external source does the unit get the most criticism?

6. From what external source does the unit get the most support?

7. In terms of resources (that is, money, equipment, staff, and so on), how rich or poor is this unit?

8. Overall, is this unit growing, staying the same size, or declining?

Concluding Questions and Remarks

1. Is there any question that I have not asked that I should have asked?

2. Thank you very much, I appreciate your cooperation.

References

Argyris, C. "Single-Loop and Double-Loop Models in Research in Decision Making." *Administrative Science Quarterly*, 1976, *21*, 363–375.

Barnard, C. I. *The Functions of the Executive*. Cambridge, Mass.: Harvard University Press, 1938.

Bartunek, J. M., Gordon, J. R., and Weathersby, R. P. "Developing 'Complicated' Understanding in Administrators." *Academy of Management Review*, 1983, *8* (2), 262–273.

Bass, B. M. *Stodgill's Handbook of Leadership: A Survey of Theory in Research*. New York: Free Press, 1981.

Bass, B. M. *Leadership and Performance Beyond Expectations*. New York: Free Press, 1985.

Bateson, G. *Mind and Nature*. New York: Bantam Books, 1979.

Bennis, W., and Nanus, B. *Leaders: The Strategies for Taking Charge*. New York: Harper & Row, 1985.

Boyatzis, R. E. *The Competent Manager*. New York: Wiley, 1982.

Burns, J. M. *Leadership*. New York: Harper & Row, 1978.

Cameron, K. S. "Cultural Congruence Strength and Type: Relationships to Effectiveness." Working paper, Business School, University of Michigan, 1985.

Cameron, K. S., and Whetten, D. A. "An Assessment of Salient Management Skills." Working paper, School of Business, University of Wisconsin, 1980.

Campbell, D. T., and Stanley, J. C. *Experimental and Quasi-Experimental Design for Research.* Skokie, Ill.: Rand McNally, 1963.

"Corporate Culture: The Hard-To-Change Values that Spell Success or Failure." *Business Week,* Oct. 27, 1980, pp. 62–70.

Csikszentmihalyi, M. *Beyond Boredom and Anxiety: The Experience of Play in Work and Games.* San Francisco: Jossey-Bass, 1975.

Daft, R. L. "Learning the Craft of Organizational Research." *Academy of Management Review,* 1983, *8* (4), 539–546.

Daft, R. L., and Wiginton, J. "Language and Organization." *Academy of Management Review,* 1979, *4,* 179–191.

Dreyfus, H. L., Dreyfus, S. E., and Athanasion, T. *Mind over Machine: The Power of Human Intuition and Expertise in the Era of the Computer.* New York: Free Press, 1986.

Driver, M. J., and Rowe, A. J. "Decision-Making Styles: A New Approach to Management Decision Making." In C. Cooper (ed.), *Behavioral Problems in Organizations,* Englewood Cliffs, N.J.: Prentice-Hall, 1979.

Faerman, S. R., Quinn, R. E., and Thompson, M. P. "Bridging Management Practice and Theory." *Public Administration Review,* 1987, *47* (3), 311–319.

Flanders, L. R. "Report I from the Federal Manager's Job and Role Survey: Analysis of Responses by SES and Mid-Management Levels Executive and Management Development Division." Washington, D.C.: U.S. Office of Personnel Management, 1981.

Forgus, R., and Shulman, B. H. *Personality: A Cognitive View.* Englewood Cliffs, N.J.: Prentice-Hall, 1979.

Gawain, S. *Creative Visualization.* New York: Bantam Books, 1982.

Gouldner, A. W. "Organizational Analysis." In R. Merton, L. Broom, and L. S. Cottrell, Jr. (eds.), *Sociology Today: Problems and Perspectives.* New York: Basic Books, 1959.

Greene, C. N. "Disenchantment with Leadership Research: Some Causes, Recommendations, and Alternative Directions." In J. G. Hunt and L. L. Larson (eds.), *Leadership: The Cutting Edge.* Carbondale: Southern Illinois University Press, 1977.

Hackman, J. R. "The Transition That Hasn't Happened." In J. R.

Kimberly and R. E. Quinn (eds.), *Managing Organizational Transitions.* Homewood, Ill.: Dow Jones-Irwin, 1984.

Hampden-Turner, C. *Maps of the Mind.* New York: Macmillan, 1981.

Hofstadter, D. R. *Gödel, Escher, Bach: An Eternal Golden Braid.* New York: Basic Books, 1979.

Hurst, D. K. "Of Boxes, Bubbles, and Effective Management." *Harvard Business Review,* 1984, *62* (3), 78–88.

Iacocca, L., and Novak, W. *Iacocca: An Autobiography.* New York: Bantam Books, 1984.

Jones, W. T. *The Romantic Syndrome: Toward a New Method in Cultural Anthropology and the History of Ideas.* The Hague: Martinus Wijhaff, 1961.

Katz, R. L. "Skills of an Effective Administrator." *Harvard Business Review,* 1974, *51,* 90–112.

Kidder, T. *The Soul of a New Machine.* Boston: Little, Brown, 1981.

Kimberly, J. R., and Quinn, R. E. *Managing Organizational Transitions.* Homewood, Ill.: Dow Jones-Irwin, 1984.

Klein, M. "Our Adult World and Its Roots in Infancy." *Human Relations,* 1959, *12,* 291–303.

Korman, A. K. "Consideration, Initiating Structure, and Organizational Criteria—A Review." *Personnel Psychology,* 1966, *19,* 349–362.

Kriegel, R., and Kriegel, M. H. *The C Zone.* New York: Doubleday, 1984.

Kuhn, T. S. "The Structure of Scientific Revolutions." *International Encyclopedia of Unified Science.* Vol. 2, no. 2. Chicago: University of Chicago Press, 1970.

Landy, F. L., Barnes-Farell, J. L., Vance, R. J., and Steel, J. W. "Statistical Control of Halo Error in Performance Ratings." *Journal of Applied Psychology,* 1980, *65,* 501–506.

Livingston, J. S. "Myth of the Well-Educated Manager." *Harvard Business Review,* 1971, *49,* 79–89.

Lundberg, C. C. "Hypothesis Creation in Organizational Behavior Research." *Academy of Management Review,* 1976, *1* (2), 5–12.

Luthans, F., and Lockwood, D. L. "Toward an Observational System for Measuring Leader Behavior in Natural Settings." In J. G. Hunt, R. Stewart, C. Schriesheim, and D. Hosking (eds.), *Managers and Leaders: An International Perspective.* New York: Pergamon, 1984.

McGregor, D. *Human Side of Enterprise.* New York: McGraw-Hill, 1960.

Mackenzie, K. D., and House, R. "Paradigm Development in the Social Sciences: A Proposed Research Strategy." *Academy of Management Review,* 1978, *3,* 7–23.

Maslow, A. *Toward a Psychology of Being.* New York: Van Nostrand Reinhold, 1962.

Masuch, M. "Vicious Circles in Organizations." *Administrative Science Quarterly,* 1985, *30,* 14–33.

Miner, J. B. "The Real Crunch in Managerial Manpower." *Harvard Business Review,* 1973, *51,* 146–158.

Miner, J. B. "The Uncertain Future of the Leadership Concept: An Overview." In J. G. Hunt and L. L. Larson (eds.), *Leadership Frontiers.* Kent, Ohio: Comparative Administration Research Institute, Kent State University, 1975.

Mintzberg, H. "The Manager's Job: Folklore and Fact." *Harvard Business Review,* 1975, *53,* 49–61.

Mitroff, I., and Mason, R. O. "Business Policy and Metaphysics: Some Philosophical Considerations." *Academy of Management Review,* 1982, *7,* 361–370.

Myers, I. B. *Manual for the Myers-Briggs Type Indicator.* Princeton, N.J.: Educational Testing Service, 1962.

Ouchi, W. G. *Theory Z: How American Business Can Meet the Japanese Challenge.* Reading, Mass.: Addison-Wesley, 1981.

Pepper, S. C. *World Hypotheses.* Berkeley: University of California Press, 1942.

Peters, T. J., and Waterman, R. H. *In Search of Excellence.* New York: Harper & Row, 1982.

Pirsig, R. M. *Zen and the Art of Motorcycle Maintenance: An Inquiry into Values.* New York: William Morrow, 1974.

Quinn, R. E. "A Competing Values Approach to Organizational Effectiveness." *Public Productivity Review,* 1981, *5,* 122–140.

Quinn, R. E. "Applying the Competing Values Approach to Leadership: Toward an Integrative Framework." In J. G. Hunt, D. Hosking, C. Schriesheim, and R. Stewart (eds.), *Leaders and*

Managers: International Perspectives on Managerial Behavior and Leadership. Elmsford, N.Y.: Pergamon Press, 1984.

Quinn, R. E., and Anderson, D. F. "Formalization as Crisis: A Transition Planning Program for Young Organizations." Paper presented at 42nd annual meeting of the Academy of Management, New York, 1982.

Quinn, R. E., and Cameron, K. "Organizational Life Cycles and Shifting Criteria of Effectiveness: Some Preliminary Evidence." *Management Science*, 1983, *29*, 33–51.

Quinn, R. E., and Cameron, K. S. *Paradox and Transformation: Toward a Framework of Change in Organization and Management.* Cambridge, Mass.: Ballinger, 1988.

Quinn, R. E., Faerman, S. R., and Dixit, N. "Perceived Performance: Some Archetypes of Managerial Effectiveness and Ineffectiveness." Working paper, Institute for Government and Policy Studies, Department of Public Administration, State University of New York at Albany, 1987.

Quinn, R. E., and Hall, R. H. "Environments, Organizations, and Policy Makers: Toward an Integrative Framework." In R. H. Hall and R. E. Quinn (eds.), *Organization Theory and Public Policy.* Beverly Hills, Calif.: Sage, 1983.

Quinn, R. E., and McGrath, M. R. "Moving Beyond the Single-Solution Perspective: The Competing Values Approach as a Diagnostic Tool." *Journal of Applied Behavioral Science*, 1982, *18* (4), 463–474.

Quinn, R. E., and McGrath, M. "Transformation of Organizational Cultures: A Competing Values Perspective." In P. Frost and others (eds.), *Organizational Culture.* Beverly Hills, Calif.: Sage, 1985.

Quinn, R. E., and Rohrbaugh, J. "A Spatial Model of Effectiveness Criteria: Toward a Competing Values Approach to Organizational Analysis." *Management Science*, 1983, *29* (3), 363–377.

Quinn, R. E., Rohrbaugh, J., and McGrath, M. "How to Improve Organizational Decision Making: A Report on Automated Decision Conferencing." *Personnel*, Nov. 1985, pp. 49–55.

Rohrbaugh, J. "Operationalizing the Competing Values Approach." *Public Productivity Review*, 1981, *2*, 141–159.

Rosenbach, W. E., and Taylor, R. L. (eds.). *Contemporary Issues in Leadership*. Boulder, Colo.: Westview Press, 1984.

Rothenberg, A. *The Emerging Goddess: The Creative Process in Art, Science, and Other Fields*. Chicago: University of Chicago Press, 1979.

Russell, B., and Branch, T. *Second Wind: The Memoir of an Opinionated Man*. New York: Random House, 1979.

Salancik, G., and others. "Leadership as an Outcome Structure and Process: A Multidimensional Analysis." In J. Hunt and L. L. Larson (eds.), *Leadership Frontiers*. Kent, Ohio: Comparative Administration Research Institute, Kent State University, 1975.

Schlesinger, L. A., Eccles, R. G., and Gabarro, J. J. *Managerial Behavior in Organizations: Texts, Cases, and Readings*. New York: McGraw-Hill, 1983.

Schriesheim, C. A., and Kerr, S. "Theories and Measures of Leadership: A Critical Appraisal of Current and Future Directions." In J. G. Hunt and L. L. Larson (eds.), *Leadership: The Cutting Edge*. Carbondale: Southern Illinois University Press, 1977.

Shepard, H. A. "Rules of Thumb for Change Agents." In W. L. French, C. H. Bell, and R. A. Zawacki (eds.), *Organizational Development: Theory, Practice, and Research*. Plano, Tex.: Business Publications, 1983.

Siu, R. G. H. *The Master Manager*. New York: Wiley, 1980.

Streufert, S., and Swezey, R. W. *Complexity, Managers, and Organizations*. Orlando, Fla.: Academic Press, 1986.

Taggart, W., and Robey, D. "Minds and Managers: On the Dual Nature of Human Information Processing and Management." *Academy of Management Review*, 1981, *6* (2), 187–195.

Thomas, L. *The Lives of a Cell: Notes of a Biology Watcher*. New York: Viking Penguin, 1974.

Torbert, W. R. *Managing the Corporate Dream: Restructuring for Long-Term Success*. Homewood, Ill.: Dow Jones-Irwin, 1987.

Turner, W. W. "Dimensions of Foreman Performance: A Factor

Analysis of Criterion Measures." *Journal of Applied Psychology*, 1960, *44*, 216–223.

Vaillant, G. E. *Adaptation to Life: How the Best and Brightest Came of Age*. Boston: Little, Brown, 1977.

Van de Ven, A. "In Search of Excellence: Lessons from America's Best Run Companies." (Book review.) *Administrative Science Quarterly*, 1983, *28* (4), 621–624.

Verdi, R. "Bears Have All the Answers." *Chicago Tribune*, Nov. 10, 1985.

Walter, G. A., and Marks, S. E. "Professional Development: Today's Experiential Challenge." *Organizational Behavior Teaching Review*, 1985, *9* (3), 1–15.

"Wasted Dollars/Wasted Lives." *Albany Times Union*, May 9, 1979, p. 1.

Weber, M. *Theory of Social and Economic Organization*. Translated by A. M. Henderson and T. Parsons. London: Oxford University Press, 1921.

Whetten, D. A., and Cameron, K. S. *Developing Management Skills*. Glenview, Ill.: Scott, Foresman, 1984.

Yukl, G. A. *Leadership in Organizations*. Englewood Cliffs, N.J.: Prentice-Hall, 1981.

Zaleznik, A. "Managers and Leaders: Are They Different?" *Harvard Business Review*, 1977, *55* (5), 67–80.

Index

Made in the USA
Lexington, KY
17 October 2012